DIGGING IN YUCATAN

DIGGING OUT THE GREAT TEMPLE OF THE WARRIORS

Bit by bit, the entire weight of the massive upper building was trans-
ferred from its old foundations to its new artificial braces.

A MAYA YOUTH BEFORE THE SHRINE OF HIS ANCESTORS

*In sunset reverie, dreaming, it seemed to me, of what might have been
had he lived in the noonday of his race.*

DIGGING IN YUCATAN

BY ANN AXTELL MORRIS

DECORATIONS BY JEAN CHARLOT

Illustrated with Photographs

DOUBLEDAY, DORAN & COMPANY, INC.

Garden City   New York

MCMXXXVI

PRINTED AT THE *Country Life Press*, GARDEN CITY, N. Y., U. S. A.

TO

LANE

CONTENTS

ILLUSTRATIONS

INTRODUCTION

To my way of thinking, archeology is the most interesting and exciting career in the world. You go places and do and see things at which no one else ever gets a chance. It means exploring and digging up buried treasure, traveling to strange countries, meeting delightful people, and best of all, finding out what was happening in the world before the first page of your history book starts. I don't care how long that volume is or how thick. Page One is no more the first page and the beginning, than W is the first letter of the alphabet. For even as the oldest pyramids of Egypt are just about twenty times younger than man-made flints found in the desert sand at their foot, so also 1492 could with more reason be used as a date for the last chapter of American history than the first. I know I used to hear so much about Columbus discovering America that I began to believe Columbus *invented* America. Not until recently did I realize that America had been a flourishing institution for centuries before Columbus was ever born, that millions of Americans had lived and died surrounded by civilized wealth and luxury before Europe accidentally stumbled upon the other, very live, half of the world.

In my search for some of this Before-History I have crawled through miles of underground caves in France to see pictures painted on rock scores of thousands of years ago, and all one summer I dug for the flint blades those same ancient folk used to kill the enormous wild animals which since have all disappeared.

I have been to the ruins of old Carthage and helped sweep the sand from a great mosaic floor set with beautiful pictures, and in that same romantic city bordering the purple African sea I have bought from a ragged little Arab child a handful of ancient coins for a thin American dime. There was a lopsided Phœnician penny thick as a wrist watch, dating before Rome; silver disks with the heads of Roman emperors upon them; and another copper bearing the portrait of a Christian bishop rubbed smooth by the fingers of the Vandals who brought great Rome to ruin.

I have climbed sheer cliffs in Arizona to caves where castles of stone stand a thousand years abandoned, and where white man's foot had never ventured. But of all the places I have been and all the things I have seen nothing exceeds in interest and romance the years I spent in the steaming Yucatan jungles where great white temples rise from a tangled deep green forest, lonely and desolated since the day Columbus sighted his first land of the New World. The treasures we found there and the adventures we met will always compose in my mind one of the most wonderful experiences a person could have.

There was our life in the old Spanish ranch house reminiscent of two hundred years of turbulent history. There was the friendship of an archeological staff and servants representing fourteen different nationalities, including the Scandinavian, as the book translators say.

There was the jaguar hunt by night when I followed the Maya Indian guide, a searchlight in his hat, for what seemed to me a trek long enough to stretch twice around all Yucatan, but resulting in not a single jaguar, although the Indians reported the next day that jaguar tracks were to be seen overlaying our own for a good part of the trip. Evidently and fortunately the animal was only mildly curious, and was not inclined to sample the flavor of North American girl.

There was a swim in the Sacred Pool of Sacrifice—a venture redeemed from frivolity only by the very real perils in climbing the perpendicular eighty-foot rock walls. The pool is the grave of countless Maya maidens who were hurled therein a thousand years ago, and has buried in its muddy floor a treasure in gold and jade carried there from half the old cities in the Americas.

There were a hundred incidents that filled those days in Yucatan, but probably none which moved me more than our very last night in Yucatan—a night of full moon, brilliant white as only a tropic moon can be, when

Earl, my husband, and I stood and looked at the great Temple of the Warriors, complete and finished after our years of work, planted monstrous and squat on its pyramid like a crouching animal, quiet with the ominous stillness of a reptile, and beautiful, but hideously so.

Four years before it had existed as nothing but a forest-covered and ragged hill without shape or meaning, but a mound that had about it some innate provocation which seized upon Earl's thought, turning him aside from other plans, almost, it seemed, bending him to its will. Nor would it release him, until after stupendous labor it had step by step returned to being—time itself turned backward—a ghostly materialization from the Land of Things Destroyed.

I had thought sometimes I would have given a great deal to be able to view life in that old temple as it was being lived before the Spaniards came. But that night I shivered in the realization of what it would mean really to see it come to life—for gorgeously decked priests to pass in solemn procession, for golden bells to tinkle and drums to throb, for the wailing of old chants to be renewed by huddled crowds below temple steps. If I would reawaken all this, at the same time terrible gods would rise up from their sleep of death—gods with the heads of poisonous snakes and the claws of fierce birds, gods who hated men and drank their blood, gods who fed on the warm beating hearts of thousands of young men, gods who smothered the New World with

Courtesy of Carnegie Institution

Fig. 1

TEMPLE OF THE WARRIORS BEFORE EXCAVATION

An unprepossessing lump of earth, which proved to contain in its heart buildings piled upon buildings.

Fig. 2   ANN AXTELL MORRIS

Who wrote this book and by means of it has tried to share with you the fascination and meaning of that most enchanting science—Archeology.

fear, and finally failed only because of the astounding courage with which they were fought by Spanish and Christian gentlemen.

Such gods are well lost, no forest can ever bury them deeply enough. But there is another and better way to read the great story of ancient times, and it is taught to us by archeology.

In this book I wish to tell something about those years spent in Yucatan and the things I learned there, for maybe you too would like to become one of those people who study archeology, finding out things about the life of ancient man that no one in the world now knows, and following the old trails over land and sea, desert and forest, canyon and plain—a life that is hard, sometimes uncomfortable, more often laborious, but one that is far too much fun ever to be called work.

DIGGING IN YUCATAN

CHAPTER I

Is There Treasure In Your Own Backyard?

A GREAT deal can be learned from the top of the ground at locations where man has once lived, when a trained and practised eye is brought to bear on the situation. Of course more can be found out by digging, just as a doctor who performs an operation on his patient has an opportunity of actually seeing with his own eyes the state of the works inside. But when the physician is sufficiently skilled he can make his diagnosis from the outside of the human shell—thumping here and listening there, using eyes sharpened by years of practice to note slight portents and signs. In the same manner, the trained archeologist, prowling over the face of the earth, can spot those slight features which mean the difference between barren digging and pay dirt. Ability in diagnosis is just as important to him as it is to the doctor.

On so many occasions I have heard people say, "But how do you know where to dig?" Now that *is* a question. It is much as if those same people inquired of a detective, "How do you catch a kidnaper?" The detective would have to write volumes to answer you fully, and then he would only be able to tell you how those kidnapers who already had done their kidnaping had been caught. But as for the unknown person who to-morrow plans to make off with Bobby Jones—the detective can no more lay down a water-tight plan for his capture than he can foretell what the weather will be like three months from yesterday. Certain routine procedure would be observed, of course, but the actual finding of the criminal would depend upon a thousand and one tiny points of fact and suppositions which shift and change from case to case. We all know that the good detective must have wide-open eyes, experience, knowledge of the human mind, perseverance, a logical brain, and enough imagination to put himself in another person's place. With that equipment he stands a good chance of finding the missing Bobby in short order, but it's a game for which he will tell you he makes up the rules as he goes along.

This situation is accurately paralleled when the archeologist stalks his prey. He too is a sleuth, and he too plays a game for which there are no set rules.

As to knowing where to dig—that's just a matter of keeping your eyes open for a clue. Every single state in our nation is littered with places where ancient man used to live. Maybe even the grass of your own backyard covers some old Indian camping ground. I believe that there isn't a single house in the United States that does not lie within walking distance of a spot where some American Indian family made its camp, fought a battle, or scratched pictures on a rock.

Sometimes the remains take the form of a mound— occasionally of a very large mound shaped like a serpent or bird or beast, looking for all the world like a huge animal cracker lying flat across field or meadow. There are many such in the Mississippi Valley, and the Before-Columbus Indians built and used them as forts and holy places.

Sometimes the old houses were dug into the ground, and so when the roof fell in it left a depression, since smoothly covered with grass and plants, but a sure clue if you are looking with an archeological eye. It isn't Nature's habit to leave holes in the ground. Man is usually responsible for a condition like that.

On occasion, arrowheads are plowed up in gardens and grain fields—a certain sign of an old camp or battleground. Remember, too, that where man lived, man also probably died. And where he died, near by he was buried. Since it was a custom of primitive man to bury useful and valuable things with his dead so that they might be used in the Happy Hunting Ground, an old Indian grave is likely to have all sorts of stuff in it that makes finding it worth while.

Caves are a good place to search. A cave was a ready-made house and saved lots of time and trouble for an Indian family. Besides, it was easy to protect against an enemy.

In rock pictures both painted and scratched, the Indians left behind them another clue. These can be found almost everywhere, literally by the million. Where man stayed long enough to do work of this sort he was almost sure to live in the neighborhood. And where he lived any length of time he was certain to leave behind him big trash mounds. These trash heaps are regular treasure troves. To begin with, our Indians were a pretty wasteful lot. They were always throwing away things that appear perfectly good to us, and even if the find is only a piece of broken pottery, it is almost as valuable to an archeologist or to a museum as a bowl that is whole.

If you should chance to come across anything that looks promising, and they are ridiculously easy to find, it would be a good idea to notify the state archeological society, because your discovery might be extremely valuable and an archeologist would probably want to see it before it was very much disturbed.

There is nothing so small that it is unimportant. For instance, a few years ago someone found near Folsom, New Mexico, a few flint spear points lying by some buffalo skeletons. Most of them were broken, and as everybody knew that Indians hunted buffalo, the whole thing didn't appear very interesting. Then an archeologist noticed that the flint points were quite different from any others ever found, and other scientists discovered that the buffalo bones represented an early type of the animal that was supposed to be extinct countless ages ago. Then there *was* excitement, because it looked as though man had lived in America thousands of years before anyone had supposed it possible. It was a clue of the greatest importance, but as archeologists will not lay down a rule from only one find, they are feverishly searching for more of the same thing. If similar conditions are found again and yet a third time, it will be completely established that countless thousands of years ago a tribe of buffalo hunters lived in America, and our pre-history will have been pushed back yet farther into the dark unknown times about which we are so curious.

There is a fascination about such work that is rarely equaled in any other pursuit. Why this is true I can't begin to tell you. There are ten thousand angles to archeology, and in various combinations some few of them appear to tempt and excite subtly almost every man, woman, and child that chances to come in touch with them. A friend of very apt wit once expressed it partially when he said that "half the human race appears to be possessed of the gopher complex." There certainly seems to be deeply implanted in us a driving urge to dig, which goes beyond reason and doesn't give a whoop whose garden is being torn up. The other half of the human race seems to be caught by the ever-fresh lure of buried treasure, by some sort of curiosity, or by the fascination of work that is neither ordinary nor humdrum—in short, work that is fun.

Yet, for all the fun, the work aspect is most decidedly present. Archeology well done is probably one of the most demanding occupations to which a person can set his hand. The true archeologist must be a master of all trades and a jack at none of them. He can't afford to slip up on a single detail for two big reasons.

One of these is that when he once breaks ground in the study of a particular location, that site is ruined beyond all help for anyone else. If he misses a single observation, that fact, and it might be an invaluable one, is lost for all time. Hence, you see, the responsibility is tremendous.

The second reason why he must be a really competent person is, from his point of view at least, a more selfish one.

A very great many of the important archeological sites now known to exist in the world are far from railroads and towns. So the venturer into these desolate districts, whether they be mountain, desert, or jungle, has to leave behind him all those things that make life easy when he is at home.

He must search out his water supply and make sure of its purity. He must serve as his own doctor in emergencies, and equally he must stand as surgeon to his motor cars which are apt to need treatment far more often than usual, on account of the terrific strain involved in departing from proper roads. He must be a chauffeur of parts who saves his cars when possible and yet who knows how, in tight moments, to adapt every ounce of power there is to his needs. He must know how to wangle his cars across bridgeless rivers without wetting the essential mechanism. He must be able to recognize the sickening feel of quicksand under his wheels and to do the proper thing inside of a split second or lose his car and all his dunnage. And not only are highways left behind, but he must be able to pick his course straight across country where not even a horse trail has penetrated.

Sometimes pack horses must be used, and often the search can be conducted only by long weary miles on foot. But in all these circumstances the archeologist must adapt his living needs to what his horse or his auto or he himself can carry. If he has an established base to which he returns year after year, and if this base can be reached by reasonably passable roads, then he can rig up living quarters that nearly approach the civilized life he has left behind. But when this is not possible, a frying pan and a blanket must stand for his hearth and his home.

An archeologist must know how to draw and to make maps, and he must be an expert camera man. He must understand the processes of preserving fragile specimens; he must have a knowledge of the physical characteristics of man, and of the geology of his district. Even botany, zoölogy, and chemistry are sometimes needed. He must have a sharp eye and a practised one for clues as to where to dig, and beyond all that he must have that feeling or sixth sense which has mysteriously directed so many archeologists to the one spot where treasure may be found. But when this faculty is dead or temporarily asleep he must show the perseverance of the steadfast ant, in trying and trying and trying yet again, until the coveted finds are turned up by shovel and trowel which neglect not a single inch of a possible site.

CHAPTER II

What Is Archeology?

Aʀᴄʜᴇᴏʟᴏɢʏ is a word that is packed as tightly full of meanings as a can is of sardines. I don't know of any word in the dictionary that has so many ideas squeezed into so tiny a space. Of course, all words are little suitcases that are neatly packed and carefully strapped until somebody thinks them or says them aloud. Then the locks break, and a hundred meanings spring out and scatter all over creation.

For instance, I say the word "dog" to you. The lid of your imagination box flies open and your own dog steps out. A brown dog, is he, or perhaps white? Anyway, there is a white dog that lives down the street, and the funny speckled dog around the corner, and the big proud chap called a St. Bernard that all the children love so much. Then there are those two breeds of snow dogs that are so different from each other—the fluffy Eskimo dogs, that people in the Far North hitch to their sleds like little horses, and the beautiful Russian wolf hounds that have developed long legs and thin bodies and great lungs in order to run faster than the fierce wolves in that far Northern country. Maybe your mind jumps to the very hot land of Mexico where are the ugliest dogs in the world, who look as if they were skinned alive, but really have learned to live without any hair coats on their bodies in order to keep cool under the fierce sun.

Straightway hundreds of dogs begin to pile out of that word box—all kinds and sizes and colors, eating and playing, good dogs and bad dogs, dogs that work for their masters and dogs that hunt wild animals, dogs that fight in wars and dogs that take care of babies, until the room is crammed full and they begin to overflow into the front yard—and every single one came out of the little three-letter word box.

That's the kind of word "archeology" is, and because it has so very many meanings it is difficult to find an easy definition of it. But for practical purposes it means finding out by any and every possible method all that we can about men of the past ages.

When an archeologist starts in to work on any one particular job he has to be equipped with three absolutely necessary tools—three tools which must be handled like dynamite, for, innocent as they sound, they possess as much destructive power as a high explosive for the site worked by the careless scientist. One is made of good hard steel, one consists of an interaction of nerves and body cells, and one has no more substance than a summer breeze.

The first one you will have guessed, for it is the spade. That is obvious because so much of what is sought lies buried beneath the ground. And yet, of the three tools, the spade should be used more sparingly than any other. An enormous amount of harm can be done by the person who rides his job roughshod—breaking and crushing his way into mounds by brute force, bent only on "treasure hunting" and going about even that so carelessly as to smash a good part of the loot he seeks, and at the same time completely destroy very valuable evidence as to just where it lay, in what position, and what objects it was near. Archeological digging, done right, should proceed with painstaking slowness, while the big crude shovels and picks should be abandoned frequently in favor of trowel and pocket knife. I have often seen soft brushes used in delicate situations—in fact the greatest treasure found in our Yucatan digging was brought to light by "excavation" with a teaspoon and a small-size watercolor paint brush!

The second thing essential to an archeologist is nothing but the human eye—although it must be an alert eye, well trained for detail work. A half-asleep eye would never do, nor one of those eyes that are looking only for the things it already believes to exist, while being comfortably blind to the bits of evidence which would tear to pieces some iron-clad theory it has already arranged with itself. The archeological eye must be as impartial as a judge and as keen as a needle, ready to note every jot and tittle of evidence that is presented to it. It has been proved possible to assist the eye with microscope, camera, and of late even with the airplane, but the eye alone is the essential device behind those mechanisms.

The third thing essential to an archeologist is so nebulous, so nearly fantastic, that I hate to mention it, although it is, in reality, of infinite value. This quality is that of imagination, and of the three it is probably the most often abused. It must be carefully controlled by such facts as are available, while remaining fluid enough

Fig. 3

Left: GUSTAV. A sturdy Norwegian sailor who came abruptly into our Yucatan life bringing clever hands, an ingenious brain, reckless courage, and a lovable personality. Whatever may be needed, be it a feat of engineering or the loyalty of a friend, one may always count on Gustav.

Fig. 4 Right: EARL frivolously suspending a deadly little coralea snake by a thread. My chiefest archeological treasure, and the best companion possible for a life of high adventure.

Courtesy of Carnegie Institution

Fig. 5

IN OLD AMERICA

*Men of copper hue, clad in skins and jewels, stood guard over broad
cities wrought from gleaming stone.*

to shift and conform as new facts are brought to light. It must be governed by stern logic and good common sense, and it must be measured out with the care of a chemist who compounds a life-giving drug. Without imagination those things which are unearthed and studied with even the minutest care remain nothing but dry bones and variegated dust, more dead than a clod of earth by the side of the road. With imagination, the broken skull from Le Moustier becomes a hideously featured creature who prowled over Europe and Asia and Africa, walking upright as does a man, making himself crude weapons with which to slay in hand-to-hand combat elephants and tigers and bears immeasurably larger than those of to-day. Neither man nor brute, he has vanished long since from the face of the globe. But from his few bones and poor stone knives the archeologist can construct a picture of the dawn of human life when man was proving with such difficulty that he had within him that power which was to conquer the earth.

It is imagination that gives life to creatures so long dead. It is imagination that rebuilds the fallen walls of ancient cities, peopling their deserted streets with long vanished races of men. That power can visualize their great trade roads stretching across the world, filled with curious travelers, greedy merchants, and soldiers setting forth to great victories or defeats now completely forgotten. On a skeleton of hard facts arduously gathered from the caves and forests and plains of the world, the archeologist can hang such trappings of vivid reality that those long dead seem to live again.

In some respects archeology is like history, but in reality it is a far bigger subject and a more basic one. The actual history of the human race is limited to a few hundred years in places like America, or a few thousand years in the Old World, while archeology carries our knowledge back tens and hundreds of thousands of years. Moreover, history is cramped into a few favored spots on the globe about which a great deal is known, and leaves the greater part of the world almost completely unaccounted for, whereas archeology pounces joyfully on these bare spots of time and space and bit by bit is succeeding in filling in the great gaps. By ways known only to himself, the archeologist can rebuild a surprisingly accurate history for those peoples who had no historian. I suppose you might call an archeologist a seeker after history. For after he makes his discoveries and fixes them definitely in space and time, they *are* history.

Take the history of Europe as an example. So many books have been published about it that we are apt to forget how comparatively recently everything told in them has happened and how limited it is geographically. North Europe did not get on the map at all till Cæsar wrote his famous book, and even Romulus and Remus themselves seem almost modern when we realize what the archeologist has to offer. His Europe goes back to the days when a rude, hardly human race filtered into the region from Asia. Huge jaws for crunching bones, apelike faces, massively muscular hair-covered bodies fit for struggle with great animals, a back-sloping forehead wherein the reasoning part of the brain had not yet found room for growth—such we know to have been the characteristics of the early Europeans, for archeologists have dug up their bones buried yards deep beneath ancient river gravels.

Wave after wave of these brutal creatures wandered over the country, and as the millenniums passed they developed increasing skill with their hands and a higher type of brain. Fire was found and brought under control; occasional sharp rocks chosen at random for weapons were abandoned in favor of flints cunningly chipped to keen edges with butts which fitted comfortably to the hand.

Finally, about twenty-five thousand years ago, a creature appeared (and nobody knows yet surely where he came from) so similar in feature and skull form to man of to-day that he comes under the heading of *Homo Sapiens*, as we do, and is quite possibly the ancestor of modern Europeans. Traces of his existence are found in exquisitely wrought flint blades, and in the astoundingly beautiful painted and carved animal pictures discovered in the deep caves of Spain and France. A search of the floors of the caves beneath the pictures revealed curious stone-carving implements which the artist had dropped when his work was complete. From these paintings archeologists realized that this particular ancient man had originated a remarkable art—of a kind which has never since been equaled. Moreover, since the artists sketched their lines right on top of previous exquisite pictures already in place, it seemed pretty evident that they hadn't worked for the sake of beauty alone. Then when some animal models were found pierced with painted darts it was not difficult to deduce that the painters believed in some old magic whereby they hoped to bring to their people success in hunting by drawing a successful hunting picture.

Earliest man lived by hunting. But after thousands of years of this hit-and-miss existence, which dictated that he perpetually wander after herds of game, he discovered that by planting a field and staying with that plot of ground he could live far more comfortably; while his dinner, which was growing in sight of his front door, wouldn't get away from him if he turned his back. It is one of the most interesting and recent triumphs of archeology that by using the airplane the outlines of those very same fields can still be traced despite thousands of years of subsequent agriculture. When a person is on the ground, the slight ridges and depressions bounding the ancient fields are quite invisible, but from the air the faint outlines are clear and lie like a map to be photographed by the camera.

Do you remember the wild forest tribes of Gaul that

Cæsar met and saw and conquered, "and the bravest of these were the Belgæ"? They were a people whom no historian had ever mentioned before they came to grips with the Romans. And yet the archeologist can tell you a great deal about them for a very long period before Cæsar introduced them to the notice of the world. They represented a cultural period in which iron was used, called La Tène, which stretched from about 500 B.C. almost to the time of the birth of Christ. This culture, which was substantially Keltic, centered in France, reached the British Isles, and thence passed eastward into central Europe. It was developed under strong Greek influence from the old colony at Marseilles, but in spite of this it remained much rougher and less civilized than the polished Greek towns. First attempts at a crude writing were being worked out and there were beginnings of fortified cities. The physical appearance of the La Tène people, their jewelry, clothing, implements, and entire manner of life are so well known that a clever painter can use that knowledge to-day to draw absolutely accurate pictures of a people of whom otherwise we would know nothing except that they put up a fight good enough to worry the redoubtable Cæsar.

This very brief account of prehistoric Europe is nothing but a thumbnail sketch dependent on a few glancing references to occasional archeological high spots. The tale in reality is lengthy and complicated, and every step is of fascinating interest. Perhaps, however, it will serve as an indication of what the archeologist has been doing in his efforts to clear up the difficult problems of what happened in the long ages before the historian takes up the story.

When a people were civilized enough to have evolved a written language, the task for the archeologist is comparatively easy. Once he succeeds in translating the old records, they automatically become historical documents and pass out of his immediate field. Some of the ancient languages are rather easy to read, such as Latin and Greek, because they never have been completely forgotten. Others have been lost to the world, but by heroic efforts their meanings have been recovered again. Egyptian and Babylonian are good examples of such tongues. But some have slipped from use, and no amount of scholarly study has succeeded in finding the key to the queer-looking signs and letters that hold the tantalizing secrets securely locked away. The Hittite letters of Asia Minor and the Maya glyphs of Central America have not yet yielded to the archeologist, though a constant siege is being maintained.

Some old writings depend on pictures instead of letters. The Indians of North America were very clever at this. For instance an Eskimo once left the following message for his friend:

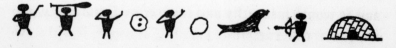

See if you can read it. The friend knew right away that it said:

(1) I (hand pointing to self) am going in that direction (hand pointing ⇒→), (2) in a boat (holding paddle). (3) Will sleep (hand at head) one night (one finger) (4) on an island having two houses. (5) Will sleep second night (two fingers) (6) on an island with no houses. (7) Am going after seals (8) with my bow and arrow. (9) Will return to my winter home.

The Aztecs of Mexico had an even more amusing kind of picture writing. They didn't draw pictures of the idea like the Eskimos, but they drew pictures of the way the words sounded. This is called *rebus* writing. If we would write that way in English we would draw a line of pictures like this

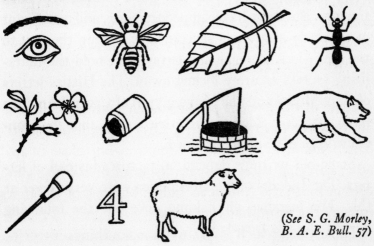

(See S. G. Morley,
B. A. E. Bull. 57)

and it would mean: "I BE-LIEVE AUNT ROSE CAN WELL BEAR ALL FOR YOU."

The Incas of Peru used a very complicated system of communication which involved tying knots in a bunch of colored strings instead of writing. They called these *quipus*. When Papa Inca got a quipu on which perhaps the first red string from the left had a big knot on it and the fifth white string had a little knot way down at the bottom, he groaned in dismay and called out to his wife, "Mama, the king wants us to pay our income tax, and the only emerald I've found this year you are wearing in your hat. Oh, what trouble!"

There are many of these quipus in museums to-day, but no one knows how to read them. There are some with numerous knots that might have been grocery bills, and some with just a single one, which may have said: "To-day was born to us an Inca boy." But the old Incas are long since gone and probably we will never know what the knotted strings truly mean. They make one of archeology's lost mysteries.

Some of the ancient people couldn't write at all, nor did they try to draw pictures. They depended on fleet-footed young men who would run from one place to another carrying their messages by word of mouth. This system made the American Indian boy one of the best runners the world has ever seen.

Those races which didn't write make things interesting for archeologists, for in order to know anything about them one has to find the things they used and left behind them so many hundreds and thousands of years ago. Sometimes enemies drove the ancient folk out of their houses and they ran away never to come back. In time the dust and sand and forest covered up everything, and it lay quietly hidden away until a lucky archeologist should come to find the city, clear out all the débris, and see exactly what the old life must have been. He enters their houses and their forts, finds pots still on the burned-out fire with the lunch only half cooked; he finds their clothes and their weapons and their jewelry; and if he is very clever he can tell you as much about the cities' owners from studying their *things* as if he found a whole library of books which they had tried to write about themselves.

It is a curious fact, and a very useful one to the archeologist, that man in all parts of the world had a bent for building again and again upon the precise spot occupied by some previous structure. The original location, of course, usually had some feature to recommend it—a great cave to offer shelter, nearness to water and rich farm lands, or a hilltop where lookouts could be posted and an easy defense planned in the face of invasion. But beyond such obvious reasoning, a site once occupied by man appears to hold a fascination for subsequent comers, and, as if it were a magnet, it attracts to itself building after building, each piled upon the débris of that one preceding it.

Nine times the city of Troy was built upon Hissarlik Hill as the fortunes of the people of Asia Minor rose and fell, and nine times it was destroyed. Certain spots in the beautiful valley of the Vézère of central France have seen more than a hundred thousand years of camp sites set up by wave after wave of the folk who poured into Europe from the east and south. There are caves in Arizona where six different culture strata can be traced, from present ground level, deep to the old floor of the cavern. In the Tigris-Euphrates Valley, the Babylonians told a legend, old even to them, of a great Deluge which covered the world. Recent digging in that region has sensationally verified the tale by revealing many layers of human occupation on top of eight feet of clean flood sand, beneath which lay the painted pottery of a people so early that only the one vague story of their existence ever survived. And London of to-day lies on top of a Roman town which in turn was built upon one captured from the early Britons which probably dates back beyond Druid days. The mother of a modern empire seems to find perfectly satisfactory the site of a barbarian river camp.

Actual dates in terms of our own calendar are very difficult to establish for ancient peoples; and they are not, although such would be interesting, absolutely essential to a correct understanding of the history of the world. It is far more important to get at their relative ages—to know which races had precedence in the districts studied and which ones were definitely later comers on the scene. It is fortunate that this very characteristic of piling cities and camps upon one another makes so beautifully clear the sequence of occupation. That one on top can definitely be described as the latest, and as the layers of different cultures are skimmed off, one by one, the order of their being is brought to light in the exact reverse order of their laying down.

Therefore, when the various types of cultures are once correctly placed in their historic order by means of related strata, even isolated instances can be instantly identified by name as representative of definite periods of time.

The importance of such findings cannot be overestimated, for it is largely by the study of stratification that archeology is raised from a rather charming adventure in guesswork to the dignity of a science.

You can see that all sorts of things go to make up archeology, and I haven't told you even a small part of them yet. It's like a great jig-saw puzzle where you have the parts lying hidden and jumbled up all over the world, and by hook or crook, by shovel and wits, you have to dig them up and fit them into the great picture of what the men on our earth looked like and what they were doing in the lost, forgotten ages before our history books begin the story we know so well.

CHAPTER III

The America Columbus Just Missed

COLUMBUS discovered America, and Columbus died without knowing that the land he discovered was a great, new, and wealthy half-world. That much is history. Columbus's diary of his voyages is a historical document, parts of which interest historians very much. However, there is one single obscure little sentence in that diary that never seemed of particular significance till an archeologist stumbled on it one day. Re-reading it in the light of his knowledge, he was able to recreate a whole story from the little incident, and from it to add another chapter to the story of that famous voyage and the resulting infamous tragedy.

If Columbus had only said *Yes* instead of *No* at one particular time he need not have died imprisoned, disgraced, and poverty stricken while other men fattened on the tons of gold from his America—gold that should have fallen to him who was the genius of them all.

Columbus stood high on the deck of his little ship and stared straight into the eye of the red setting sun. He was thinking of home. Spain was far away, the ocean was very wide, and the path was undoubtedly beset with those terrible great sea monsters which he had heard could lift horrible toothy faces as high as his own topsails and smash a Spanish galleon as easily as wet crumpled paper. It was true that he had been very lucky about sea monsters so far. This was his fourth voyage across the Sea of Darkness, and I believe that he was the only sailor in Europe who didn't tell "true stories" about the great serpents which rippled over the water's surface like gigantic angleworms, long as a king's palace and big around as seven fat oxen.

Columbus was a very brave man but it was hard to think of possible sea serpents, and storms, and weeks upon weeks of dreary sailing between himself and the home he loved. He was old and tired and just a little discouraged. His men were homesick and mutinous. Every day they came to him and begged him: "Sir, we have found enough. Why do we sail further? May we not now go home? What care we for the gold of the Indies if we never see home again?"

Home, home—the word beat about Columbus's head. Why not turn now? His heart swelled at the thought of his friend the good queen Isabella. Why waste more time sailing around these dreary and endless waters? Home it should be. He raised his voice, "Helmsman, we——" but a hoarse shout interrupted: "A boat, a boat, sir." The helm was put hard over and the empty sails flapped with a deafening clatter as the ship lunged to a stop, barely avoiding crashing into an approaching boat.

I'm afraid the lookout was dozing, but months of sailing the only ship on the Atlantic Ocean had very naturally dulled his vigilance. The entire crew rushed to the side to see what manner of bark this might be, and found themselves being stared at with no less curiosity by a dozen bronze-skinned fellows who were paddling an enormously long canoe hollowed from a single great tree. Under an awning spread in the center reclined a gorgeously clad chieftain who looked at Columbus with a pleased and royal astonishment.

Who knows what he thought as he looked at the Spanish ship with the great cloth sails, and at the curiously dressed fair-skinned European? Did that dim legend which all America seemed to know, about a "fair god" of white skin and blue eyes who had come to their shores in the far past bringing great gifts and help to their people, but who had sailed away promising some day to return—did the memories of that old story stir in his mind?

His eyes flashed with pleasure, he stood erect, and laying his right hand upon his heart—a gesture of peace and good will—he spoke gracefully in greeting. There was some little confusion at this. The chieftain's singsong monosyllables sounded strange on the European ear. Columbus shook his head in puzzlement and questioned in the Spanish dialect of Castile, "Who are you and whence come you?" The stranger's great black eyes looked blank. Other dialects were tried, and Portuguese and French and Italian with no better success. Finally a gunner was summoned who had lived long in India and knew the language of that country. This surely would be understood by a native of India, he thought. But when the final measure failed the two men stood staring at each other with puzzled smiles, quite tongue-tied.

As a last resort, the language of signs was used and then things went better, for the stranger made it clear that he was inviting the Spanish ship to visit his home to the westward and that he wished to do honor to the men. Columbus strained his eyes into the fast-darkening west but could see no land. He liked the tall kingly stranger—he was drawn to him far more than to the scrubby "Indians" he had met on his first island landing at San Salvador. He looked calculatingly at the canoe and found it large and commodious, and amply stocked with food and tall jars of water. To his mind this meant a long voyage and a great distance from land; he was quite forgetting that without a European compass it was a rare and foolhardy mariner who would venture very far off shore. If the stranger could only have made him understand that he was but returning from a lengthy coast-wise journey, and that the shores of his great country, prosperous and wealthy, were but a few miles distant!

Curiosity fought a short and losing battle with the previous thoughts of home. Columbus shook his head abruptly, turned to the helmsman, and finished his interrupted sentence: "We will sail eastward—we are going home."

Columbus died not knowing that his little Bahama island was half a world away from India, and the disappointed stranger chieftain returned to the shores of the great American mainland with nothing but a fantastic story of "a winged tower floating upon the sea and filled with white-skinned men in shining clothes."

Columbus had been invited to visit America and had refused the invitation!

Archeologists have ascertained that this happened off the coast of Yucatan, therefore our chieftain was a Maya, one of the richest and most powerful people in America. A guest of a Maya king could have taken a shipload of presents to the greedy Spanish courtiers and could have presented Queen Isabella with a New Indies of ten times the value of the Old. By so little did Columbus at the last miss his great reward.

Those old diaries and letters make thrilling reading to-day. The tales of battles and plots, of gold and precious stones, of American kings and Spanish conquerors fascinate as much by what they leave untold as by what they actually say. Every now and then some new document comes to light and then we have one more link to the great chain of the story of old and vanished America. Some of the tales are gross exaggerations, some break off tantalizingly in the very midst, but from the tangle the archeologists are gradually pruning and gathering those things which may be taken for fact.

Following Columbus's first great step towards the Unknown, it seemed as if all of the captains of war and sailors in Europe streamed out across the Sea of Darkness to explore and gather the wealth of what they still called "India" by this new short route.

After all, the Western Sea appeared to have no dangerous edge over which ships would tumble to fall forever into the great endless space which made up the

Not-World. As you know, before Columbus the world was supposed to be quite small and flat as a plate, without any rim around the edge, so if unwary persons sailed too far in any one direction they could very easily slip right off and never come back. It had happened more than once. Of course nobody had ever actually *seen* anybody else struggling in panic upon the brim of the world, but sometimes an occasional ship had blown far away into the Western Sea and had never come back. The sea serpents undoubtedly accounted for a few, but as for the others—the old sailors whittling their bits of wood on the docks of London and Genoa could tell fearful and quite-to-be-believed stories. It was hard for them to stop · believing the old tale in spite of Columbus's news—it is always very hard for old people to stop believing things.

Wrinkled old Sailor Thomas was certain the new gossip wasn't so. He knew. When Ferdinand Magellan was a little boy he remembered how the old sailor used to tell him that he had seen with his own eyes birds and fish which left the forests and streams around his village every year and came back again without fail the next season. The very same nightingale with the torn left wing, and the wise old salmon with the hook caught in his gill. If the world was so big and round why didn't they go on and on to new countries? No, sir, they went to the edge of the world and then *had* to come home because there was no place else to go. There was no doubt about that!

But little Ferdinand Magellan was very young, and it's always easy for young people to believe new things. When he grew up and he and his friends had sailed his ship into the Sea of Darkness and on and on till they had sailed quite around the world, and came back home from the other direction, the bells of Lisbon rang out in wild joy because Portuguese boys had believed and done such a new thing.

After a while men knew that this wide new land which lay stretched like a great wall down the Western Sea could not possibly be India and so they called it America. They found America to be a wonderful country where millions of strange folk lived who knew no more about Europe than the people of Europe knew about them. They had brown skins and straight black hair and ate strange new foods—potatoes, cornbread, cocoa, beans, peanuts, red pepper, squash, tapioca, turkeys, and, best of all, popcorn with maple syrup. These foods were very good indeed, and after a time there wasn't a woman in Europe who thought she could prepare a decent meal without imported foodstuffs from America.

The strange Americans that the Spaniards found in Mexico and Central America and Peru had built great cities full of high temples to their gods and painted palaces for their kings, and they dressed these kings in gorgeous and beautiful clothes made of the feathers of thousands of bright-colored tiny birds. They had great armies which carried strange weapons, and their wise men knew secrets of the stars for which Europe had been searching for centuries.

But more than all of this, the Americans had gold and precious stones—wealth beyond the wildest dreams of the kings of Europe—emeralds and jade piled into open baskets and carried around like cucumbers; gold so plentiful that it was used for garden spades, and more bars of raw silver than there were donkeys' ears in Europe.

All this wealth turned out to be a sad thing for the Americans. For them gold was nothing but a soft yellow metal—"sun metal," they called it—that was easy to melt and hammer into the shapes they wanted, but it meant far different things to Europe. You see, gold in itself is nothing but a kind of metal very like iron and lead and really not half so pretty as a piece of rainbow-colored glass. There are three things to be done with it: You can use it for a beautiful ornament like a bunch of flowers; you can trade it off to somebody else for *things* —things to eat and things to wear and things to play with; or you can hold it like a terrible whip and with it buy great power—buy the work of people's hands, buy years of their life, buy the right to make them do your will, and even buy their very bodies. Gold can be a very good or a very terrible thing. America was gold-innocent but Europe was gold-wicked.

Europe **went** mad over American gold. A Spanish

servant wrote home to his master a long letter about America which the don put carefully away behind a secret panel in an old Spanish palace where it has just recently been found. In this letter the boy says: "It is the richest land in the world. It has so much gold innumerable or without comparison, and has much silver and precious stones. One can hardly tell what wonderful things one finds in their houses."

After the first long gasp of startled surprise the Spaniards fell upon this wealth like a pack of starving wolves. They tore it from temple walls, they grabbed the jewels from the necks of the kings themselves, they even snatched a little golden toy from a baby playing in the street. The friendly Americans at first glad to welcome the strange travelers in their homes and generous in their gifts to the queer race of White Skins who seemed so crazily mad over their yellow metal, were astounded and terrified, and finally furious over such treatment. But by that time it was too late for them to help themselves. Their kings were killed or captive, their forts were held, their cities were in flames, and the Spanish flag waved over half America.

The tale of the capture of the great cities of old America makes one of the most astonishing true stories ever told. Pizarro, a Spanish swineherd who had never learned to write his own name, captured the 3,000-mile-long Inca Empire with only 200 men, and in seven months carried fifteen million dollars' worth of gold in thousands of back-breaking loads to his ships. Cortez landed in Mexico with 450 men, sunk his ships so there would be no turning back, and in a few months' time a million Aztecs and all Mexico fell under his rule. These Spaniards were brave beyond anything ever seen in this world. Greedy they were and sometimes cruel, but as an example of sheer courage they have to be admired. Luck played mightily into their hands, but it was their own wits which knew how to take advantage of such amazing fortune.

America in their hands was a treasure house to be looted, and painfully thorough they were about it. Whole kingdoms and empires were wiped from existence that the Spanish king might triumph. The recovery of the history of these lost rulers and their people, the folk who were truly Americans, is of intense interest to us secondary Americans of to-day, and to this task the American archeologist has dedicated himself.

CHAPTER IV

Why We Went to Yucatan

W E BEGAN learning things about the archeology of Egypt a long time ago—about the Pyramids and the mysterious Sphinx and the tombs of kings. We were even more interested in Greece and Rome, perhaps be-

cause those peoples were so very much like us of to-day,
and because their history is really the beginning of our
own. But until a very short time ago no one knew much
of anything about what really had been happening in
America before the Europeans came. When we thought
about the American Indian we usually remembered the
friendly Massasoit bringing turkeys for a Pilgrim
Thanksgiving, or the wicked painted savages who came
out of the great woods to flourish tomahawks for a few
short years, and then seemed to vanish like blue smoke
from the face of the earth.

The old stories of great temples and tropical treasure
didn't seem real, nor did anybody concern himself to
find out what the Spanish hullabaloo was all about.
Then strange travelers' tales began to filter into the
newspapers, people kept digging up queer things on their
farms, occasionally news of a mummy was heard, and as
a result of it all, curiosity about American history before
the schoolbooks take it up started to simmer and boil.

Scientific men began to work at the question system-
atically, and they found that the longer they studied and
dug and hunted, the more complicated the problem became. They collected thousands of things for museums,
but they discovered they didn't know where the first
American had come from, or when he had appeared, or
why he had come at all. They couldn't figure out why
there seemed to be so many different kinds of Indians,
all doing so many different kinds of things. They tried to

find out how the Indians had moved great building stones in South America which weighed tons without wheels or animals to help, and how they had made the thousands of tiny beads found in New Mexico, which were no thicker than a Christmas card and no bigger than a pin head, without machinery or even metal tools. They puzzled over unpleasant little Chinese insects found in Peruvian mummies' hair when the Peruvians themselves weren't Chinese at all; they worried over Central American astronomers who worked out a far better calendar than the one in Europe, although they had no telescopes, and they concocted a hundred reasons to account for the fact that when the Spaniards came, the Mexicans fought them with exactly the same complicated kind of weapon that had gone out of fashion in Europe ten thousand years before.

In fact, as they worked, the puzzle seemed to get more difficult instead of easier. So they decided that the only way to go about the matter was to stop trying to fit all of the broken bits of information together at one fell swoop but for each group of archeologists to study just one place at a time until absolutely everything was known about it, and then to work near-by places in ever-widening circles until some day the whole pattern would fall into order and meaning.

Not more than a dozen blocks from the White House stands a gray stone building. It is the home office of the

Carnegie Institution of Washington, D. C., an organ-
ization which exists for the purposes of finding out a
great deal concerning the things of which mankind now
knows but little and of discovering other things which
are entirely new. In a room that looks down on busy
Sixteenth Street sits one of the wisest men in America,
Dr. John C. Merriam. All day and often far into the
night there come to his desk the reports of the specialists who have gone to the ends of the earth in search of
some special knowledge about the earth itself, the sun,
the stars, or the creatures and men that live upon the
earth.

Each year for a very long time Dr. Sylvanus G. Morley had been sent to Central America by the Carnegie
Institution to learn all he could about the jungle-hidden
ruined cities where once lived the Maya people. You
will remember that it was a Maya chieftain who had
vainly besought Columbus to come and visit him in one
of those great towns that now are only heaps of stones
overgrown with great trees and thorny, creeping vines.

The Maya had a wonderful system of hieroglyphic
writing, unlike any other writing which any other
people ever used or invented. And they had a habit of
writing not only on a kind of paper, but also on stone.
Of course, most of the paper decayed long ages ago, but
the stone has lasted as only stone can. That curious
writing Dr. Morley can read as easily as you and I this
very page of print.

Season after season Dr. Morley fought his way through the jungles of southern Mexico, Yucatan, Honduras, and Guatemala to read the dates at the Maya cities which had already been found, and each year he found cities that white men had never heard of before. Some day he planned to dig out the ruins of one of those cities, and he was on the watch for the grandest and the finest of them all. Many a night as he lay in his hammock swung beneath forest trees, his body wrapped like a mummy in cheesecloth to keep out the ants and ticks and scorpions, or as he tossed and sweated in his bunk in some tramp steamer on his way home, listening to the cockroaches running up and down the walls, a whole host of Maya cities passed before his mind—Chichen Itza, Copan, Quirigua, Palenque, Piedras Negras. Queer names they are to us, but to Dr. Morley each one meant a spot as familiar to him as his own front yard. Always his mind went back to Chichen Itza, where finally, one day in 1914, he decided he would dig, and Dr. Merriam approved his decision.

Of all those tongue-twisting names, there is only one that I want you to learn to pronounce, because that is the city about which this book is written. Chichen Itza —*not* "chicken itza," as some people insist on spoiling it—is correctly pronounced with the heavy, slow Maya drawl Cheé-chen Eet'-za'. It is made up of a group of Indian words which mean "The Mouth of the Wells of the Itzas." The last word is the family name of the kings who ruled one branch of the Maya for hundreds of years before, during, and after the period of time they dwelt in the city itself. There are two very large wells, which are really deeply sunken lakes, at that place; and since water is very scarce in Yucatan, the discovery of these pools made possible the development of a large city around them. The pools were so remarkable for their size as to give the city the name it bears to this day.

Yucatan itself is easy to find on a map. It is a large peninsula branching from the lower southeast part of Mexico, thrusting itself like a huge thumb out through the Caribbean Sea toward Cuba.

When we first find traces of the Maya (pronounced My-ya) race, they are living south of Yucatan in the jungle lands now crowded by many scrappy little Central American republics. How long they had been there we do not know definitely, but it was long enough to build a series of cities ornate with marvelous sculpture and architecture. The earliest written date from the New World comes from this southland of the Maya, and has been interpreted in terms of our own time count as 68 A.D. Now that is only relatively old, of course. It leaves a moderately long period to be accounted for, until the coming of Columbus and the early Spaniards— an interval for which we do know the main outlines of history; but it leaves also completely to guesswork the far longer period which must have preceded it.

There are two ways that we have for estimating this

unknown stretch of earlier time. One is based on the fact
that the culture of the first dated period, 68 A.D., in all
phases of its development is of a very high order, while
preceding it, and under it, is recorded layer after layer
of older remains classed as the Archaic. This earlier
culture shows such definite affiliations with the Maya
civilization that undoubtedly it was ancestral thereto.
As yet, we have no idea for how long an interval this
Archaic horizon continued, nor what could have preceded it, since it is not crude in itself.

The other reason we have for believing the 68 A.D.
date to be late in Maya history lies in the extraordinary
calendar from which it is derived. This calendar represents an intricate and astonishing feat of pure mathe-
matics, which dealt in theoretical time cycles 30,000
years long, and yet could fix with almost absolute
accuracy any single desired day within this vast interval. It was far more accurate, indeed, than the system
under which the so-called civilized world operated, until,
about a century ago, the Revised Gregorian Calendar
was put into effect. Such a calendar was not invented in
a week. Untold years of laborious calculation, coupled
with inspired vision, must have been necessary to bring
it to the finished state where we find our first date.
Hence these years, too, must be reckoned with when we
look back toward the lost beginnings of the Maya
people.

Maya culture reached its highest point in the south.

Then, for some unknown reason, things began to go to pieces. The bolder spirits packed up bag and baggage, completely abandoned hearth and home, and started on the move. As to what happened to cause this mass migration, no one can tell. Whether some dreadful sickness broke out, or the land became weakened under unskillful farming, or grasshopper plagues ate the crops, or civil war broke out, or some ancient Bolshevism began to gnaw into an obedient people's lives—any of these might account for it.

At any rate, the Maya pulled up stakes, and must have wandered in the wilderness for many times forty years; because when eventually they started building again—this time in Yucatan—they marked the first sites with dates reading about 450 A.D.

Chichen Itza came to be one of the great capitals in this new land. For a thousand years it flourished before the Spaniards came. Here, some sixty miles inland, a crowded knot of temples and palaces rose above the plains of Yucatan. Within the palaces native rulers held sway over hundreds of thousands of people whose homes spread away to the seacoast both to the north and east, and a great distance inland toward the west. On the edge of the city there was, and is, a huge natural well which was a shrine to the Gods of Rain. To that shrine came pilgrims from the whole of the Indian world for a thousand miles away to cast their sacrifices into the black-green waters of this pool. The Spanish conquerors wrote down many tales about the wonders of this city as told them by the Indians. All these Dr. Morley had read, and besides, he knew much more about the city from the old manuscripts of stone which he himself had deciphered. He could hardly wait to see and to tell the world about the wonderful things he felt sure were hidden by the tree-capped mounds of stone that marked the spots where once the great white temples gleamed in all their magnificence.

But there was a long and tedious wait ahead. The Mexican government has very strict laws about its antiquities, and no work of exploration among the ruins within its territories can be undertaken by a respectable institution without a definite agreement with the government as to terms and conditions. Dr. Morley began negotiations with the officials in Mexico City.

The Mexican people are very proud of the accomplishments of their ancestors. The blood of the Mexican nation is mostly Indian, diluted with only a little bit of Spanish, so that the people of to-day are really the many times grandsons of the ones who built the ancient cities. Rightly enough, the Mexicans resent the work of those who come only to dig and to carry away what they find to the museums of a foreign country. But the Carnegie Institution had no such end in view. All it wanted was to study the ancient ruins; to bring away maps, photographs, and descriptions of them so that books could be written about them to tell anyone who cares to read something of the glories of one of the greatest of ancient American civilizations. Everything that it found was to be turned over to the Mexican government, and the institution was willing to repair the buildings it excavated, so that they would stand for years like exhibits in an out-of-doors museum.

The Mexican officials were willing to grant the Carnegie Institution a concession to dig at Chichen Itza. But it always takes a long time to think over all the things that must be touched upon and included in a contract of this sort. Before Dr. Morley could get a concession definitely signed a great revolution broke out in Mexico. During a civil war no one mixed up in it has time to think about ruins, and if there were time there would not be much use entering into a contract with whoever seemed to have the upper hand, because if the other side were to win, then of course the contract would not be honored. Moreover, the new officials would regard such a person with suspicion because it would appear that he had been a friend of their enemies.

For years one revolution in Mexico was scarcely ended before another one began, so all Dr. Morley could do was to wait. Finally there came a time when it seemed as if there were peace in Mexico which might last. In 1923 a concession granting the Carnegie Institution the right to explore the city of Chichen Itza was signed. Then Dr. Morley began to look about for helpers, because in the great task that lay ahead, the work of many minds and many hands would be necessary to carry it on successfully.

Here is where I come into the story. My husband had begun to play with a pick and shovel when he was barely big enough to carry them around. And in all the years since then he had continued to think of them as playthings, instead of tools for hard work as most people regard them. As a result, he had learned through long practice to use a shovel as skillfully as an artist can a brush, and to workmen he could teach some little of that skill.

He had played among the prehistoric ruins of New Mexico as a child, and he had explored so many of them for the University of Colorado and the American Museum of Natural History of New York since he had grown up, that the problems of excavation were as simple to him as our A B C's. He could look at a pile of fallen stones and tell just where the walls ran beneath them, and how to go about clearing out the filled-up rooms with the least labor and expense. As for finding things, he combined the instincts and abilities of a hungry dog after a rabbit with the sure force of a powerful magnet acting on a handful of tacks. If he could not find an ancient grave, a piece of buried pottery, an arrowhead, or a turquoise bead, then those who knew him, knew also that such things were not there.

Back in 1912, he and Dr. Morley had dug together in the Maya City of Quirigua in Guatemala. So one day a letter reached our camp, which was beside a great pueblo ruin in New Mexico, offering Earl Morris a position as Director of Excavations on the Chichen Itza Project.

In December, 1923, we went to Washington, for where Earl went I went also, preparatory to outfitting for the first season's work at Chichen Itza. Just then another revolution broke out. Days became weeks and weeks lengthened into months while we cooled our heels and devoured the newspapers for word of the Mexican struggle. Eventually the revolution failed, leaving in power the faction which had signed our concession; the concession, therefore, was still good. One day at the end of April the glad news came in a wire from Dr. Morley:

Leave to-morrow on Crescent Limited for New Orleans to outfit for Yucatan.

CHAPTER V

New Orleans to the Temple of the Plumed Serpent

By that time the season was so far advanced that we couldn't hope to do very much work that year, but it was a splendid opportunity to get things started for the years to come. We knew that Yucatan doesn't have a summer and a winter as we have in the United States. They have wet and dry seasons. The dry seasons are so hot they sizzle, but the wet seasons are drowned in rain—not showers or even storms, but tropical rain like nothing on earth but itself. The sky simply falls in solid chunks of wetness. Sheets of water roll off the roofs for weeks without stopping. That's not the kind of weather you can do anything outdoors, and certainly not the kind of weather fit for archeology. The Rains (and they are justly capitalized) begin about the middle of May, giving you vicious little spats about once a day, then soon twice and three times, until finally one rain hasn't even begun to get ready to stop before another has well started. By December it all stops as suddenly as if turned off at the faucet, and Yucatan begins to bake and broil like an overdone pancake in a hot oven, with never a wisp of water to cool it.

The heat was uncomfortable but the rains were impossible, so we hurried our shopping in order to get off as soon as might be. Canned food, tropical clothes, sun helmets, tools, and all the things we thought we might need were bundled on board a tramp freighter. Not much was needed for so short a season, but through the following years we found that hundreds of tons of material were to prove a necessity to us. It took an imagination amounting to genius to figure out ahead of time everything that would be absolutely indispensable as the work went on.

Finally we were all tucked on board with a disgraceful

amount of baggage—trunks and suitcases packed to the
bursting point and the overflow consigned to cardboard
boxes and paper bags, very much like a Sunday-school
picnic. Space seemed a trifle constricted, but before we
had time to complain very loudly, forty frightened cows
arrived on the dock all neatly tagged for Yucatan. It
was a case of "Move up in the front of the boat, please,"
and we shared what little room there was with our forty
bovine passengers. The whole of that trip was one solid
haze of cow. Cows to the right of us, cows to the left of
us, but mostly cows to the windward!

A night and a day and another night and another day
and yet another night went by—hot, dull, odorous
hours which ran even slower because of our eagerness to
arrive at the journey's end. Then a morning when the
queer, tremendous silence of stopped engines was succeeded by hammering on the cabin door—"Breakfast
served"—which in turn was drowned by a terrific
blast on the whistle—"Captain calling for a pilot, sir."
We dressed in haste and tumbled out on deck.

Since that day I have been down to Yucatan five
times, but I never seem to lose the thrill of seeing the
stretch of dazzling beach, the green coconut palms
against a bright blue sky, and the long line of pink and
blue buildings in the port of Progresso, Yucatan. It is a
sight which always brings back the old excitement of
tropic shores, strange peoples, mysterious lost cities, and
buried treasure.

Our heads were full of splendid practical plans. We would land early and take the inland train in the cool of the morning, and thus escape the heat. Good plans, but they didn't match with unfolding facts for a nickel, or perhaps, now we are so near a Mexican shore, I should say five *centavos*.

To begin with, the last revolution I mentioned was intended to be a rough native copy of the famous one in Russia, and when the tidal wave subsided a few Russian ideas were left stranded high and dry on Mexican shores. One outstanding product was the making of Progresso into a Soviet, a microscopic but real Soviet-blood relative to Moscow itself. This measure of freedom quite went to Progresso's head and she straightway proceeded to pass a thick book as full of laws as would quite strangle a more experienced government. The greatest interest of Sovietism seems to be in laws about work—that is, to keep people from doing too much work, which might seem an unnecessary activity in itself. But such care for its leisure suited Progresso very well and the residents were evidently practising up the morning we arrived.

For a much longer time than it has taken me to tell it, the deafening whistle blasts were kept up while the captain called for the pilot. No pilot. Finally our steam ran out, and new fires were built to provide voice for calling the missing pilot. Another hour of hooting went on while we sat on our luggage and wished we hadn't packed the deck of cards. Then the captain, who was Irish and whose face was getting a good deal too red, ended up a long description of his feeling toward pilots and announced that he would dock the ship himself. This he proceeded to do, drawing 'longside the wharf very skillfully in about ten minutes, and called to a dock hand to catch the rope and give it a turn about the post.

Everyone always likes to catch ships' ropes. It gives people a lovely feeling to tie down a thing so much bigger than themselves. The man on the dock forgot all about the laws of not working, made a joyful grab, and promptly found himself in lots of trouble. Up rushed a very much gold-braided somebody who yanked out a wicked-looking revolver, aimed at our luckless helper, and said in substance, "Who touches a strand of yon hemp rope dies like a dog." Then, turning the gun our way, he employed it to emphasize a long flow of eloquence to the effect that the Progresso harbor was too dangerous for amateur pilots, and even though we had made it safely, it was against the law, and that we had to go away again and he didn't want to have to lay eyes on our ship until it was decently equipped with domestic pilot or pilots, and that in the meantime he would take the dockman to jail (for wanting to work, we gathered), and that he would take us all to jail too except that it wouldn't be legal without a pilot.

Our captain nobly suppressed any inclination to chat

further, whispered gently down the tube to the engine-
room, "Full speed astern," and back we went into the
Gulf of Mexico and took a long ride we hadn't paid for
round and round in a circle—I imagine just so we would
have the sensation of going somewhere.

Every time we swung into the arc of the circle nearest
Progresso, our whistle would bellow and shriek for a
pilot, but whatever the reason was for his non-appear-
ance before, now it was only too evident that he was
depriving us of his person as a punishment. The noonday sun grew broiling hot, and we ate the last scraps
of food on board for lunch, taking comfort in the thought
of cases of soda crackers and corned beef packed with
our expedition's material in the hold.

About two o'clock the pilot boat was seen rowing out
from the pier and excitement ran high on board. You
may remember I said the captain was Irish, and no
Irishman is ever too mad to be witty. He waited till
the rowboat was nearish, then he backed the ship a
trifle and stopped again to wait. As the rowboat drew
closer a second time, he backed slowly some more, and
continued the game until he lured the poor suffering
rowers miles out to sea, while they, who had no land-
mark on the open ocean to judge by, didn't realize what
was happening. Finally we let them come alongside,
only to receive a last most crushing blow. For the pilot
hadn't come at all; he had only sent his office boy with a
note to say he would come after he took a nap!

When that day was over we had learned a great deal about Soviets, we had landed in Yucatan, and after facing a battery of immigration authorities, customs men, and doctors, we had caught an evening train for Merida, the capital city of Yucatan.

There was no time for sightseeing on that occasion as we were scheduled to leave Merida at five o'clock the next morning; that meant getting up rather uncomfortably early. We found in all our later travels in Yucatan that trains always leave at that before-sunrise hour so they can get where they are going and back again before dinner in the evening. It's not such a bad idea either, because they are the most strictly uncomfortable trains I ever rode on, and I can't blame the engineer and conductor for wanting a square meal and a good night's sleep before having to start it all over again.

The little engines burn wood at an enormous rate. The quantity of sticks it takes to boost them to a trotting speed or a downhill gallop is appalling. We've often mentally congratulated the railroad on running through so many thick woods that have an ability to grow fast between cuttings. The fuel is stacked beside the track every few miles, and by the time each pile is dry enough to be picked up and burned, the cutover ground is well on the way toward being a forest again.

The rate of plant and tree growth is one of the amazing occurrences of the tropics that you have to see really to believe. I have watched with my own eyes a great banana leaf, which in the early morning presented itself as a tight green cylinder about six feet long, unroll by visible jerks until at noon it had flapped fully open. And I remember the time when some bean and cement sacks broke open and spilled their contents on a freight-car floor. Some economical person carefully saved the cement, which was made into sidewalks later, but the few intermingled beans, rejoicing in tropical heat and rain, proceeded to grow in their cement beds as enthusiastically as in soft and carefully prepared gardens at home.

On this trip the train was loaded to the gills with travelers and their luggage. Although our car was labeled *First Class*, it soon began to resemble a poultry show. Evidently no self-respecting Yucatecan would travel without a certain number of live fowls—chickens in baskets, turkeys in sacks, geese tied up in the family bed linen, and a bird or two carried carelessly in the hand instead of suitcases.

After Merida was left behind, the train bumped along for hours over a country as flat as a pancake griddle and planted as far as eye could reach with orderly rows of sisal or *henequen*. This is a plant that looks a little like some forms of the cactus. It has long sharp bayonet leaves which are ground up and dried into a fiber from which rope is made. The old Mayas who built the city we were going to work in had grown the same plant a thousand years before and had found it and the country well adapted to one another. Yucatan to-day exports thousands of tons of it to the United States, and finds that it brings back wealth to a country otherwise rather limited in produce.

The great red sun rising upon the scene shone through the shifting tropical mists, green in tint, almost as if color-soaked by the plants on which it had rested during the night. Soon we brought up with a crashing halt at a little village of pink-washed houses with straw-thatched roofs and surrounded by whitewashed walls.

Our train was besieged by native women and children bringing food to sell. As breakfast had been rather sketchy, the prospect of something to eat sounded pretty good, and when we found what there was, we were even more tickled. The trays were piled high with hot *tortillas*, flat native corn cakes patted thin as cardboard and filled sandwich-fashion with deer meat. This was new indeed, and yet at the same time a food as old as the forgotten pyramids. We had read about it in the letters of the Spanish soldiers, and now was a chance to step back a thousand years to eat the same breakfast as a Maya emperor. We bought one each—a sort of romantic tryout—but after the first bite I nearly fell out of the window reaching for more, and digging into my pocket for Mexican coppers. No wonder the Maya had never changed their style in breakfast foods! Those deer-tortillas were among the best things I ever ate.

A blowing of whistles, and we were ready to start

again. Everybody braced himself against the nearest solid object and held his breath till the engine could get our not-too-round wheels to turning again. An agonized moment of waiting, then, *Wham*—something burst and the little train clattered off, leaving our car stranded and dead as a door nail. Some excited little boys set off to catch up with the engine—I must admit it wasn't very difficult—and it backed gravely into its original place. As the fireman, who had quite evidently dealt with similar emergencies before, climbed down off the tender, he brought a slender stick of firewood with him which he jammed into the place of the broken coupling pin, gave it a kick which evidently satisfied him as to its ability to meet all demands, and off we started in triumph.

More towns and henequen fields and forests filed past, each looking exactly like the last until we were fairly hypnotized by repetition. Then came the long-looked-for station of Citas and we piled out, counted our forty pieces of baggage for the next to the last time, and began to wake up to the duties of taking an active part in the stationary landscape.

The expedition's chauffeur was there to meet us. Pablo was a square little Maya who had climbed high enough in the social scale to leave poultry carrying behind him and to flaunt proud ownership of one of the oldest Fords that had ever seen light of day at Detroit. Unbelievably patched tires, broken lights, and a starting apparatus which worked automatically enough after ten minutes' hard cranking were some of its more obvious defects. When the engine was running, queer sounds met the ear which seemed to bear no relationship to the usual process of a gasoline motor, while the only possible manner of stopping it, once it was under way, was to disembowel the ignition and short circuit a raw wire end against the steering post.

But these were minor faults, considering that the car was equipped with the most gorgeous and shining poly-chrome effects I had ever seen. Pablo had been for-warded some money to put his car in good running order, but in keeping with his own taste in motor equip-ment and in honor of the Carnegie Institution, the entire sum had been devoted to upholstery worthy of a Rolls-Royce. The scarlet leather trimmings alone proved this to be a Ford beyond all value and worthy of the most exacting comparison with those in the United States.

Our speechlessness in the face of the spectacle was interpreted as bedazzlement. Nor was Pablo altogether wrong. Five of us and a goodly amount of baggage were stowed away and we set off on the last lap of our jour-ney into the interior. This manner of travel made obser-vation a bit easier, and we felt we were becoming better acquainted with the hot flat land where we were to live so long.

We found the life to be extraordinarily similar to that

reported by the Spaniards in 1500, but one accidental occurrence suddenly upset those thoughts of such relatively recent antiquity. A tire blew out, and while we perched on the side of the road watching repairs, across the brow of a short hill immediately before us there waddled an unbelievable monster. It was really only an *iguana*, a reptile measuring about three feet in length, but one which in casual appearance was an exact and miniature duplicate of the dinosaur, extinct a million years ago. High back crest, long spiky tail, lowering snout of hideous look were all outlined in the heat waves against the sky, and from our position so near the ground's surface we had for the moment no sense of real size or scale. The thing was a gigantic dinosaur to the life. Lizard though it was, the family likeness was much too close for comfort and for the moment it made us feel very small and exceedingly prehistoric.

Under way once more, and I for one began to shiver with excitement at the thought of coming so near to our goal. A last corner was rounded, and instead of another blank vista of unchanging forest, a clear straight road led for more than a mile straight to a sight of breathtaking beauty. A great white pyramid towered high above the forest, capped by a squat and massive temple. A moment of stunned silence, then we all simply burst into garbled jumbles of English language and began pounding one another deliriously.

Chichen Itza and the end of the road at last! This was what the Spaniards had seen! No wonder they had written letters full of superlatives, in a vain attempt to describe what was indescribable. And in the future it was to lie with us to search with the eye of scientific archeology till we might see more than the Spaniards ever had in 1500. At the moment we didn't know it, but we were to turn back the pages of time from that date and find that city after city had been built on this same ground. We were to uncover temples which lay in ruins before Columbus was ever born, and to find treasure that had been buried and forgotten while the Roman Empire was falling into decay. And we were to bring to people who could never go to Chichen Itza a knowledge of its beauty and its wonder.

CHAPTER VI

The House of the Three Kings

My DILEMMA at this point is like the one that troubled me the day I first arrived at Chichen. For while now I do not know what to describe first, then I did not know what to see first.

I felt exactly like the excited Spanish soldier who, on approaching Chichen Itza for the first time, found he couldn't contain his curiosity another minute. He broke ranks and hurrying up to the stately leader asked, "My lord, what manner of a city will this be? Is there a king at Chichen Itza?"

What manner of a city would it be? There was no king at Chichen Itza—of that I was certain. His Majesty was long since departed, but just over the hill I could see the crest of a splendid pile of masonry that surely could be nothing less than his palace. I determined to explore straightway. Down a faintly marked path through the bush, around a corner, and there before me stood a great structure utterly different from the temple-capped pyramid I had first spied on the approach to Chichen. High it was, built upon a tall, straight-sided rectangular base that rose fifty feet above my head.

I was to find in my future wanderings that it was customary for the Maya to build on the top of artificial hills laboriously constructed by their own hands. Yucatan for the most part is literally flat as a table, and completely covered with forest. Therefore, in order to give their temples and palaces the places of importance they deserved, the builders cheerfully undertook to supply what Nature had neglected to provide. For almost every structure, they proceeded to build their own mountain, rearing it high above the trees, facing it with smooth stone and carving it with strange figures. And not until that stupendous initial labor had been completed did they lay the first block of their four walls.

Broad steep steps led to the top of the foundation. They were rather ruinous in condition and further complicated by the Maya idea of the proper manner of building a staircase (Fig. 8). Instead of constructing a step wide enough for one to plant a foot on it with safety, and the rise to the next sufficiently low for a comfortable step-up, they made the treads so extremely narrow that a person has to ascend them sideways, crab fashion, and they made the risers so high that it is difficult to keep one's chin out of the way of one's knees. The finished product causes the climber to feel as if he were ascending a ladder without any hand holds for that satisfactory life-and-death grip. I know I hugged the steps so tightly with the soles of my feet, curling my toes so violently on that first trip, that by the time I got to the top my outraged muscles refused to unkink themselves for a few moments, and I developed a magnificent "charlie-horse" cramp, which for several days made me feel as if I were tottering around on glass bones.

I sat down on the top for a short breathing space and from that height could see all Chichen spread out before me. The sight was very much like one of the airplane photographs taken by Colonel Lindbergh in 1929, when he made his exploration flight over Yucatan. I had a map in my pocket—one that was marked with all of the temples and buildings that anyone then knew about—

and unfolding it I began to figure out just where I was, and what the buildings were called that I could see dotting the bush near and far.

So my building that I had just painfully conquered was not a king's palace at all! The Spaniards had named it the Monjas, or Nunnery, and although they presumably knew why, not another detail had they given.

The great trouble with writing letters and books is to say all those things that will be interesting to your readers, and to leave out the dull, boring stuff that people already know, or don't want to know even if you try to tell them. When the Spaniards wrote about Chichen Itza they left out far too much. One little phrase, a name, or a brief story of something that happened they gave, and we who planned to study the city down to the last detail had to fill out the gaps as best we might. It was far too much like a huge game of hop-scotch, with our imaginations leaping vainly over the vast blank ground that remained unmentioned. Even the incident that I told at the beginning of this chapter, of the soldier who inquired "Is there a king at Chichen Itza?" comes at the bottom of a sheet of paper, and the next page, which would have answered and settled that question beyond all doubt, appears to be forever lost. It is true that we have our suspicions as to whether there was a king at Chichen Itza in 1544, but I'll tell you more about that later, and you can see what you think is the probable answer.

Oh, those careless Spaniards, with their lost letters and unwritten books—if only we might uproot them from their moldy graves and shake from their brains those precious facts they knew and allowed to die with them! How we did puzzle over the name of the Monjas. Was it called a nunnery merely because to a Spanish eye it resembled one of those great religious houses of the homeland, or did a group of maidens really live there shut away from the world, and if that is true, what story or curious custom accounted for them?

A second stairway, shorter in length, led up from the platform where I was resting, but I determined first to examine the stage I was on before tackling any more Maya steps. The terrace was quite broad and appeared completely to surround the building planted upon it. This second story was carved from tip to toe with a beautiful lattice work design in stone, and near the top, the walls sloped back slightly to meet a flat roof. There were rows of doors upon the two long sides and one small room at either end. Most of the rooms were exceedingly tiny, with no openings except the single narrow doorway. Originally the entrances had been closed with woven cloth curtains, though of these nothing now remains except the small grooves at the top and bottom of the door jambs, indicating where they were hung and tied shut. Such bare-walled, cell-like rooms admirably bore out the Spanish idea of a convent.

But on the far side I suddenly entered a great long

Fig. 6 *Courtesy of Carnegie Institution*

THE CASTILLO—TEMPLE OF THE PLUMED SERPENT

A great pyramid towered high above the forest, capped by a squat and massive temple.

Fig. 7

AN OLD PALACE, IN WHICH THE SPANIARDS WERE NEARLY TRAPPED WHEN THEY CONQUERED YUCATAN.

The story of their escape is one of those delightful tales which go to make up solemn history.

hall with a vaulted roof covered with tantalizing bits of a colored picture. This had been a grand room indeed, and I immediately recognized it as the one I had seen in photographs taken by that great English scholar, Maudslay, who in 1888 had made a long stay in the city during his Central American explorations.

Mr. Maudslay and a friend had made their head-quarters in this room, partly I imagine just for the fun of it, and partly because it offered such a cool, well-protected shelter against the rather violent Yucatan climate. After arriving at Chichen, however, they had both come down with bad bouts of malarial fever, a disease which makes a person feel just about as ill as he possibly can. It is a curious symptom of malaria that the fever attacks one only every other day, while on the days between, a certain very welcome, though weak-kneed, rationality intervenes. Fortunately for Mr. Maudslay, he and his friend were afflicted on alternate days, so one of them was always enabled to care for the other in constantly changing nursing shifts.

As he tells the story, water was the greatest problem, for romantic as their self-instituted hospital was, it was situated almost half a mile from the great natural well which offered the only water supply. However, that mile walk to the well and return was only the least of the invalid water carrier's troubles. The well, or, as the Maya call it, *cenote*, was a natural great pit about one hundred and fifty feet wide, with the water level seventy feet below the surface of the country. The walls were almost sheer and the only method of descent was by a steep rocky trail, narrow enough to make a goat nervous, forest-darkened, and slippery with tropic damp never reached by rays of the sun. After this perilous ascent, overladen with the heavy burden, there remained the terrific flight of steps which I had just climbed, a last bit nearly enough to break their fever-pounding hearts. Blazing sun, shaking limbs, slopping bucket—the exhausted carrier would finally drag himself to the crest with only a few inches of tepid fluid remaining to make up for half a day's cruel effort.

The second flight of steps led to the flat top of the rooms through which I had just been rummaging, and there I found the ragged fragments of a little building which didn't amount to much. It had evidently been stuck on as an afterthought, and had been constructed of pieces of carved stone picked up here and there, all over the city, and thrown together without any pattern arrangement. It looked very like a sore thumb, and later I was to learn that such tacky little structures were an evidence of the days when Chichen was failing in power, and possessed no strength or energy to attempt the large, beautiful work characteristic of her great days.

There was only one interesting thing about this little building and that was a tiny tower at the top of the staircase which carries with it an amusing story. It seems that when the Spaniards invaded Chichen Itza, they had rather a hard time of it at first. The natives put up a stiff fight for their city and in the course of it the Spaniards took refuge on the top of this very Monjas. You will remember I said the foundation was high with straight walls, and the staircase was so steep it was an easy matter to defend the building from attack. The Itza folk, however, knew how to play a waiting game, and they sat down to keep an eye on the steps until the Spaniards needed a drink of water badly enough to come down and get it.

A few days went by and the Spaniards became desperate. They knew they had no chance, a mere score of men against an army thousands strong. But they were shrewd, as they well had to be, to conquer whole nations with only their handful of troops. So one night the leader, with offers of meat, coaxed a hungry Maya dog up the stairs and tied him to the bell which he had hung in the little tower to use for mustering his men in case of attack. Then he put bits of meat all around the dog just out of reach. The poor animal spent the night rushing at his rope's end from one side to the other in a vain attempt to get his supper, and of course the bell put up a fearful clamor. The Mayas thought it signified an attack, and while they watched assiduously the empty staircase, the Spaniards slid down a rope onto some rough ground at the back of the building and slipped silently away in the darkness. When morning broke, they were twenty miles distant and the Mayas were treated to the sight of an empty fort held only by one of their own miserable dogs.

That is one story the Spaniards remembered to tell— probably because they thought they were so clever about it.

From the Monjas the path led a bit further to one of the prettiest, neatest, most up-to-date "ruins" I had ever seen (Fig. 9). It was very like the Monjas in general style, although much smaller, but it was in such marvelous condition that it looked as though the inhabitants had moved out only yesterday. After climbing the short flight of steps to the terrace, I found myself tiptoeing to the door, because my feeling was so strong that maybe the owners hadn't really left at all, but were only sleeping.

The place was as bare as Mother Hubbard's cupboard, however, although slick and clean as a new pin. I found from my map that it had been named the Chi-Chan-Chob, or "Strong Clean House," but was now called the Casa Colorado or "Red House" on account of a band of red paint on the walls of the main room, and was reported to be the "best preserved ruin in America." Well preserved it certainly was, but not much more ruinous than the Grand Central Station in New York. It was touching to think of that perfect little stone cottage having stood lonesome and empty for centuries, deserted even by the lizards.

One long room extended across the front of the house through the back wall of which three doors led into three absolutely identical little rooms. A living room and three bedrooms, of course. My mind jumped irresistibly to the Three Bears, but then, realizing that those popular animals probably never had lived in Yucatan in the course of their earthly careers, I suddenly remembered an old Maya story about three kings of Chichen Itza. They were brothers, and nephews of a wicked king who ruled vast estates. As little boys they played about the palace and had great sport in the forests near the city. They were absolutely inseparable, loving each other far more than most brothers. They hunted deer and jaguars and grew strong and healthy. They went to school to a wise old priest, and being extremely smart boys, they learned to read the queer, long, folding Maya books very quickly, although they had to spend an unconscionably long time over their arithmetic. (Maya arithmetic was probably the hardest in the world. Lots of grown-up archeologists are working on it to-day, and there probably aren't five of them that are as good at it as those three little Maya princelings.)

They went into the army together to learn the business of soldiering. The Maya royal family had to know everything there was to know, and had to be ready to do anything there was to do. They were supposed to be rulers, judges, priests, teachers, astronomers, and captains of war. Rather a strenuous education, you must admit.

Everywhere the boys went they were liked. They were clever and kind and brave, and their people adored them. However, as so often happens when an unusually intelligent man is educated to be king, he becomes dissatisfied with the old-time methods of ruling and thinks and plans great schemes for making things better. The three princes used to talk for long hours about how to make their people happier, and about the right way for kings to live. They felt that a king should take more care than an ordinary person to be a good man, because his subjects were so apt to imitate his actions.

They realized that their uncle was not setting a good example. The poor people of Chichen Itza were suffering on account of the terrific amount of work they had to give to palace and temple building while their corn fields became choked with weeds. The great palace itself had been changed and enlarged eight times, one right after the other. Four generations of workers, for nearly a hundred years, had been forced to do little else but laboriously cut stone and carry it from the quarries for this one building, while their own hut roofs leaked and their children cried with hunger. The rich nobles, on the other hand, followed their king in his cruelty and carelessness, and spent their time in frivolous pleasures and greedy feastings.

After a time the wicked king died, and the people came rejoicing to the eldest of the three princes to give him the crown. But this boy, who was now a

young man, didn't want to be torn away from his dear
brothers even to be a king. If he were to wear the Itza
crown, he knew that it would mean a separation forever
from the good old days when they three had lived and
worked together, each on an equality with the other
two. He didn't want Tui and Dak to kiss the ground in
front of his throne. Why, the three of them would never
be able to keep from laughing, and that would be shock-
ing on solemn occasions!

So he explained a little of his feelings to the people in
a grave and royal manner, as a prince should, but they
were broken-hearted. Then one bright fellow had a
grand idea. "Let all three brothers be king!" he shouted,
and straightway the people broke into glad uproar.
The great question was settled at last, and so all three
were crowned on the dawn of the Maya New Year's
Day.

It was the dawn of a New Year indeed for Chichen
Itza, and the three brothers ruled so well and so kindly
that their lives, instead of falling into a forgotten
nothingness, are remembered to this day. One of the
first things they did was to give the great palace, which
had cost so much in work and gold, to a band of holy
maidens to use as a home. And on the door was carved
in Maya letters the date of that happy New Year, which
on our calendar is 1019 A.D. The date is still there, and
even now the building is called the Nunnery.

A tiny house, a miniature of the old palace, was built

for the three kings, with three little bedrooms just alike and a long hall which they all used together as a throne room and judgment hall. The three brothers are long ago dead, but the wide-open doors and the clean bare rooms are still waiting and ready in case some day Chichen Itza's beloved kings come back.

Fig. 8   Courtesy of Carnegie Institution

Fig. 9   Courtesy of Carnegie Institution

THE HOUSE OF THE THREE KINGS

*One of the prettiest, neatest, most up-to-date "ruins" in America,
whose wide open doors and clean bare rooms have been watching these
many centuries for Chichen Itza's beloved kings to come back.*

Fig. 10

DESCENDANT OF AN ANCIENT MAYA PRINCE

Standing in the doorway on the Astronomical Observatory. This was the building wherein the high priests used to calculate the date for planting crops.

CHAPTER VII

What Happened in the Court of the Thousand Columns

THE most interesting part of archeology lies in the things you have to dig up for yourself. Fascinating as the Monjas and the House of the Three Kings were, the fact remained that there was not enough left to find out about them. All you had to do was to walk up the steps and in the front door. That was too easy.

But there were scattered throughout the city innumerable untouched mounds, big and little, and completely covered over by a ruthless forest which had no more compunctions about growing on top of a fallen sacred temple than in any other more normal place. If the roof and walls of a building once collapse, seedlings find it only too easy to take root in the tumbled mass of mortar, earth, and stone. The same climate which enables beans to grow lustily out of a new cement walk provided a regular forcing house for the great trees which sprung out of these mounds. The roots bore down through the stones, disrupting and bursting whatever might have remained intact when the top of a structure fell, to an almost complete annihilation of a one-time beautiful and large building. Now, after generations of forest have grown and fallen into decay on the spot, all that remains is a shapeless, earth-covered mound with only an occasional glimpse of a cut stone to suggest ancient magnificence.

Our map maker, Jerry Kilmartin, had been at work for months before we arrived, not only recording the well-known standing buildings, but doing special work ferreting out these unknown mounds. It was a terrifically difficult job, since he was required to cut every step of his way through a tangle of trees and underbrush with a *machete*, that wicked-looking bush knife which in

Central America serves every possible need, from a table utensil to weapon-in-chief in the business of war and revolution. In the northeast part of the city he had traced out a very large complex of mounds which appeared to surround an open plaza about five acres in extent. The tops of long lines of stone columns were visible, while, attached to these alignments here and there, a steep and ragged pyramid slope pushed above the column level.

This court had hardly been touched since the day it had at last given up the losing fight against the marching wall of forest. No mention of it had ever been made by the Spaniards, nothing similar to it had ever been found in America. This truly, we thought, would prove the best place to start investigations. So our hordes of workmen gathered from the near-by villages were turned loose upon the tangled vegetation. Trees and bushes were cut and stacked in the center of the court and one fine day were fired. The huge column of flame rose straight in the air, as if to meet with the sun itself, while Jerry, who was working on his maps a quarter of a mile away in the bush, and who didn't know about the bonfire, wiped his streaming face and muttered disgustedly, "I didn't know even Yucatan could be this hot!"

When the flames died down, we returned to our court to see what we had, and to talk over ways and means of tackling it. It seemed dreadfully big, now that one

could really see from end to end of the great column
ranges and could look across the vacant square much
larger than a baseball field. What a job it would be! Not
even then did we have the slightest realization of the
complications and wonders that future years of digging
would reveal. The tops of many columns showed above
the mold, others lay sprawling in the court with broken
drums, and we had to estimate from the building pattern the position of some as well as we could figure it.
We counted them—eight hundred, nine hundred; then,
just before rounding back to the starting place, the
grand total of one thousand. And so the place received
the name by which now it is so well known: The Court
of the Thousand Columns.

Subsequent digging, though even now not nearly completed, revealed it to be a hollow square surrounded by
a stone-roofed colonnade four columns deep, broken in
the front by a gateway and pierced on one side by an
underground tunnel which led, back-door fashion, out
into some rough ground beyond the city limits. It was
flanked by temples and pyramids, while the central
cleared area was dotted over with scores of tiny low
stone platforms.

It is a very impressive building group, but the purpose
of its construction is a great puzzle. Not the slightest
hint of legend remains to enlighten us. It had undoubtedly fallen into decay before the Spaniards came, because surely they would have remarked upon such an

enormous and unusual piece of architecture. One could as easily visit Rome and completely ignore the Forum.

It is a case for pure guesswork, and your opinion will be as good as mine. Let me reconstruct for a few minutes, build back the fallen stones, replace the heavy roofs, and with a finger dipped in the paint of old Maya stories change its desolate loneliness into the vivid, moving pageant lost a thousand years ago. Perhaps, if we coax an old Itza king and his crowd of subjects back through the main gate, they may once more take up life where they dropped it, and by watching carefully what they do, we may be able to determine to our satisfaction their reason for building the Court of the Thousand Columns.

Let us have it about four o'clock in the afternoon in the year 1250, when Chichen Itza was beginning to stir awake after the usual long siesta taken during the heat of the day. The sun's rays slanted against the great mystic pyramid temple built to the Plumed Serpent God, throwing a creeping and monstrous blue shadow over the glaring white plaza until it became tangled among the myriad columns and was thrown back against itself prismatically, on the colored striped inner wall of the great court built to the east.

At the first touch of the cool shadow two soldiers guarding the gate of the court sprang to startled attention. They had been sharing the city's nap, but none but the practised eye of their top sergeant would have known it, for they had learned to reduce the art of duty to a perfect science of deception. There was nothing for them to be vigilant about now anyway. Almost a hundred years had passed since their people had come down from Mexico to help the King of Mayapan beat back the too-ambitious Itza kings into their proper place. They had been given Chichen Itza as their part of the spoils, and for a while there had been many a bitter conflict between the people of the city and their foreign conquerors. From soldiers they had turned into policemen, but after a time the antagonism gradually died down and the conquerors themselves were peacefully conquered, as so often happens. They began to look on Chichen Itza as their home. Bitterness changed to a half-jovial teasing, and soon the two races were working side by side as if they had always been friends.

The guarding of the gate was only an old custom which had lost its meaning, but the city was by this time so tied to the habit that it never occurred to anyone that there was no real reason why their soldiers should roast in the blazing sun during the long afternoon hours. The guards themselves, however, had arranged matters so they wouldn't be cheated of their siesta. They braced themselves each against a column, tipping back their heads slightly so that the thickly plumed blue helmets wouldn't betray them into top-heavy nods. Then, as a final measure of precaution, they took shelter behind their spears. They had borrowed the Maya custom of adorning their spears just below the hafted point with heavy clusters of feathers and these they held upright by thrusting them through their knotted belt loops and balancing them between the toes of their sandaled feet. Behind the protective feather screens thus afforded their faces they could snooze to their hearts' content, standing bolt upright, and no one be the wiser.

Soon people began to file across the plaza and through the gate. Among the first were two tall, handsome young Maya chaps, one of whom was carefully balancing a stone jar of liquid black paint in his hand. They hailed the soldier to the left: "Hello there, Snubnose, what's the news?"

The soldier snickered, "If I had a nose like a parrot's beak, as some people do that I could mention, I wouldn't be so proud of it."

"Tut, tut, General—or is it only Captain?—I can't remember. His Majesty himself is the only man in the country with a longer nose than mine. By the gods of my ancestors, you can't run around like this criticizing an Itza nose that has been important for hundreds of years before you ever sniffed the light of day with those stubby little Mexican nostrils of yours. Why don't you get the High Priest to change it for you? He told my father last night that he'd heard of a new way to cure headaches by cutting out a piece of the skull."

The soldier spat out a piece of tattered sugar cane

and snorted, "Well, to my mind, the High Priest is spending too much time on these newfangled notions of doctoring, and not enough on his astronomy. For two weeks now the farmers have been coming in and cluttering up the city, waiting for him to give the word to start planting crops. If he doesn't watch out the sun will pass the sacred point on the horizon and then it'll be too late to get them in before the rains."

"Yeah? Well, stop worrying, soldier, I've never seen the army go hungry yet. Anyway, I heard him say that he was pretty sure that soon the sun would strike the two necessary points through his observatory window. It was only a bit off yesterday. You might spread the word so he'll have a good audience. The old man likes a lot of attention."

"Well, what are you getting so hard-boiled about?" drawled the soldier. "I thought you just ate up those temple ceremonies. That's the stuff you paint, isn't it?"

"Oh, how old-fashioned and unesthetic is our army," sighed the artist. "That's out-of-date now, and you're the last man in the Maya Empire to find it out. That's the stuff my grandfather used to paint, you mean. He drew strings of imaginary priests and soldiers so long that if you laid them end to end they would reach from here to that Mexican home you pretend to be so proud of but have never seen. We young fellows have different ideas. We're going to paint real pictures of real people actually doing things. I've got an idea now that's a perfect corker for doing a picture of that amusing little town on the coast where we get our fish. The chief architect is going to let me try it out on the walls of the new temple over there. *Your* new temple, I should say. Did you know they are going to call it the Temple of the Warriors?"

"Did I know it! Say, young fellows, the army knows everything except about Art, and that's nothing anyway."

"I respect your wisdom, sir, but if it's possible to teach you anything new, though I doubt it, come on over to the temple when you're off duty and Chan here will sculpture your portrait and give you a taste of immortality. Soldiers have been known to die, you know, but Art is eternal. See you later."

The two young artists ascended the low steps to the long open colonnade and sauntered its length toward the new temple where they were both working. A word or two was exchanged with friends on the way, for all of leisured Chichen Itza appeared to be gathering for an afternoon's chat.

"You know," our talkative painter addressed his companion, "my father calls this the real Whispering Gallery of the city. Of course, the architects of the great Ball Court are proud of the way a whisper will carry from one end of their walled field to another, but a lowly murmured piece of gossip starting here seems to run from one end of the town to the other in a split second. However, we're late; better hurry up."

Two more steps up and they entered the new colonnade which lay across the foot of Warriors' Temple. A sterner place, this. The stone cutters were just lowering into place a small shaped block in front of a luridly painted altar. It was a sacrificial stone over which would be stretched the screaming victims of the ominous Maya religion preparatory to having the hearts ripped from their living bodies.

The artists ascended the steep stairs to the crest of the pyramid whereon the temple was built and, passing in the great serpent-door, proceeded through to the building's back room, or Inner Sanctuary. Little light streamed through the single narrow door into this dark and windowless chamber but torches were lit, and by their flicker the painter saw a good half dozen of his rivals busily at work covering the great walls with colorful patterns.

He made a face, whispering to his companion, "Do you know, the more I see of artists the better I like myself."

"You couldn't like yourself any better, Tuche. Not even the Fair God himself could be more resplendently beautiful or more extraordinarily clever than you think you are."

Tuche was astounded and hurt. "But my dear Chan,

you must be ill or something. I thought something was wrong, you've been so silent. Come on, let's look at the work you've been doing, and I'll try my best to bow down in admiration before old-fashioned art. That ought to brace you up."

Chan replied bitterly, "Well, if you can imagine any subject besides the same old warriors and priests that I could fit onto these high, narrow column faces, I'll give you my best jade necklace. Twenty columns I have to do; every one has four sides. Can you imagine anyone trying to rush through eighty human-figure representations and make them all different without getting ill or something?"

"Chan, you're a great artist, but you have absolutely no imagination. I can think of a lot of things you could sculp on a column twelve feet high and two feet broad. Why don't you try an exceptionally long-legged heron drinking the falling rain?" He whooped in sudden laughter. "Can't you just see the High Priest if you did? He'd have a thousand fits."

While the two artists settle to work, let us leave the temple and, following to the high back corner of the pyramid where it looks down into the Court of the Columns, overtake the Chief Architect while he surveys his latest handiwork.

The painters had not yet begun their work on the exterior walls which stood clear and white in the lengthening sun's rays, and looked as solid as a mountain of cut rock.

"A good job, well done," he mused. "It ought to last forever. Though I'm not too sure of those wooden beam supports for the roof. The spread of the arches is too wide and the roof too heavy, but for that matter we never could have found stone beams that would have served. I wonder if a better roof couldn't be devised. The way we've been building, with a roof heavier than the supporting walls, isn't sound." For a moment the vague shadow of an inspiration crossed his mind—something about bracing the two sides of an arch against a stone at its crest, a block that would serve as a key to the terrific stress of heavy weight—then with a puff of evening breeze it was gone, and from his vantage point he fell to figuring on the new range of columns with which the king wished to enclose completely the side of the court already partially flanked by the Temple of the Warriors.

The builder's dissatisfaction was well justified. He touched upon his temple's one weak point. The dead weight of a roof thrice as heavy as the understructure, while the chief of those supports were composed of a material which rotted easily as does wood, was the sole reason that we found a pitiful tumbled mass of broken masonry on the site where once reared his glorious temple. Whereas if that notion of the true arch, on which the architects of the Old World had based its permanent monuments, had been fully matured, instead of dying after flickering for a brief moment in his thoughts, his buildings would have endured even as have the Gothic cathedrals which were raised in the same century half a world away.

In the meantime, down below him the crowds milled in a murmuring mass through the court, like slow-moving white-clad insects. Many of the people were doing the day's shopping in the numerous temporary booths scattered over the court. Some of these little shops had stone floors and straw thatched roofs, and a few of the better ones were covered by swaying cloth awnings which were supported by poles thrust into stone standards set firmly into the masonry foundation.

All manner of things were being bought and sold in this rather informal market. It supplied the city with both luxuries and necessities, combining the functions of a complete department store with the color and strangeness of a far-eastern bazaar. What tourist of to-day wouldn't beggar himself in an hour if he could have but one chance at that old Chichen Itza market!

There were curious fruits, and parrots that talked Maya, and great hand-woven tapestries dyed in old reds and glowing yellows and rich vegetable blues. There were hammered-gold plates ornate with scenes of battle, jewels wrought of turquoise and jade and pearl, bells of soft pure gold, and cloaks of feathers or the

supple skins of the black-and-yellow spotted jaguar.
As for money, our tourist could put away his American
dollars or English pounds. All a buyer needed in those
days was a handful of coco beans or a string of the small
red shells; with that coin he could fill his boxes to overflowing with those things which are to-day almost
priceless in the museums of the world.

But I am afraid, even as to-day, the things that were
beautiful received scant attention, while the stalls of the
food merchant were crowded. There were the poor
people, always hungry, jammed around the shops where
corn and black beans and high-smelling dried fish were
sold. And there were the servants of the plump rich
who vainly searched for tid-bits with which to stuff
further their gluttonous masters. They bought tender-
loin of baby fauns, the breasts of gamey wild turkeys,
iguana tails, and that best of all desserts—*calabazas
meladas*, which was made by piercing hard-shelled
gourds through to their squash-like hearts with dozens
of tiny holes, and then boiling them in great vats of
syrup and honey till the meat of the fruit was soaked
in the rich sweetness.

Toward sunset, great numbers of the farmers, whose
fields were long miles beyond the city limits, were
restlessly gathering around the steps of the royal palace,
which opened into the Court of the Columns on the
south, hoping that this night the God of the Sun and the
Planting would speak at last through the High Priest

and permit them to get back to their work. No man might plant before the sacred moment or his crops would be burnt by the vengeful sun, nor might he delay beyond that date or his tender seedlings would be washed from their beds by the torrents loosened by the God of the Rains. The necessity for nice calculation in this matter is evident, and since mathematical astronomy was confined to the priest class alone, the farming economics of the empire had devolved into a solemn rite wherein the original true point was quite lost, even to the priests themselves, in a misty tangle of religious significance.

Inside the Royal Palace there was dire trouble. A spirit of anxiety afflicted the rigid guard, the busy servants, and even the gardener who was watering the plants of the small central open court in the cool of the day, so that the fierce sun should not boil the moisture around the roots and thus kill instead of nourish. The Itza king and the High Priest had been closeted alone together for hours, and the murmur of voices occasionally rising to heated high words had drifted through the curtained door.

Inside the tiny stuffy council room the argument rounded ceaselessly back on itself in a vain attempt by one of these two lords of Chichen to impress his point on the other. The subject of their argument concerned those very farmers who by this time had jammed the big court outside to overflowing.

"But your Highness, can I move the Sun God himself? Another night, maybe two, and the moment of planting will be revealed on the observatory stone. Can you not wait a little while?"

To which the keen-eyed king by a heroic effort of control smoothly replied, "Your Holy Reverence does not appear to understand. I have explained what a dangerous time this is for the empire. The working people are restless. Strange ideas are filling their minds. They resent conscription in our wars; they are refusing to pay my taxes; they are even murmuring against my person itself. While they labor they have no time for foolishness, but idle, they are a greater menace than even the plotting of the City of Uxmal."

"This I realized," answered the Priest. "But the farmers are not dangerous as are the folk of the town. It is always the cities which are the hotbeds of revolution."

The Itza flinched. "Stop—I don't like that word! But as for that, I have kept the town busy enough, forsooth, in my ceaseless projects of building. I have enlarged the Temple of the Warriors to twice its original size, and now that is done, I have decreed a new colonnade to flank its side." He chuckled. "The Chief Architect resents this a bit, because it will cover up a lot of carving on his temple and he sees no reason why it should ever have been done at all. He doesn't realize that I am frantically working against a social dry rot that, if allowed to persist, will tumble his temples to the ground and destroy far more than a few yards of carving."

"But where then do the farmers come into this?" the High Priest stupidly pressed his argument.

"Where, where indeed?"

The Itza rose to his feet, his cold tones shaken with exasperation.

"Where would thousands of idle men, choking the city streets, gossiping all day, rioting all night, fomenting turbulence—where would they come in? Look to your altars, old man, for my throne will not totter alone! This has happened before. Rid me of these farmers and that straightway, or by all the gods, the Itza kings and the Itza priests will be homeless once again. Hang your observatory and your sun and your calendar! Tell those men to go, and to go to-night. Lie to them! Then, if you must, feed your annoyed gods with human sacrifices till they are glutted, even as my fat lazy nobles, and too stuffed to care!"

Thus did the canny Itza labor against the paralysis of tradition, and unknowingly prophesy. How heavy would have been his proud heart if he could have stood with Earl and myself on the crest of the tumbled mound that once was his brand-new Temple of the Warriors and looked over the burnt-out emptiness of the one-time busy market, across jagged rows of broken stone marking the stately colonnades, to the vacant sunken heap of rock where his palace walls had collapsed into the midst of the carefully tended garden.

Earl turned to me. "This court must have been wonderfully beautiful once. I wonder what it was used for."

CHAPTER VIII

Our Workmen

As a first step in our excavations, the two gates were cleared in order to facilitate the traffic movements of trucks and wheelbarrows. While this was in process Earl and Dr. Morley carefully went over the entire

Court of the Columns, building by building, mound by mound, almost inch by inch, searching out the salient features, investigating the relation of the buildings one to another, and as far as archeologists might without the help of pure magic, reading from slight surface indications the secrets that were buried below the ground.

Chichen Itza was strange to them both. Not only were the actual problems of Yucatecan architecture a little-worked field, but the question of workmen loomed heavily. Exploration of the dimensions that this court would involve required not only a larger staff of directors and specialists than was at hand that first season, but in addition laborers for the actual pick-and-shovel work had to be recruited from the country round about. They had to be trained, organized under captains who were to be chosen, and the unfit had to be weeded out.

Whenever natives of a foreign country are selected for labor, great care has to be exercised. The whole point of the work must be made clear in order that there may be intelligent coöperation, wages must be correctly proportionated, and local feuds, racial quarrels, or what not must be carefully avoided.

The first step lies in securing a head man, or *major domo*, to whom a large amount of responsibility can be delegated. This man must be an executive and a politician, wise in his dealings with his men, honest in his relations with the staff, intelligent both in human contacts and actual work. Moreover, he must be a resident of the district in order to be in touch with the problems of the workmen, and he must speak the language both of his directors and of the country.

It is a large order, as you can see, and we were fortunate in finding the very man in Juan Olaldi, a dignified old Mexican, foxy as a serpent, who had served as major domo on a Chichen plantation for forty years. Both Earl and Dr. Morley had a fluent Spanish as a result of earlier years of work in Central America, and Juan spoke as easily the Maya tongue, a language older than the pyramids among which we were to work.

Through an admirable wiliness, Juan had managed to steer clear of entangling alliances with either of the two factions of the Chichen neighborhood. The near-by village of Piste was a hotbed of banditry, and the whole district was divided along cleavage lines which embraced every imaginable social and economic subject, but which in the end might be said to boil down to a case of bandits who were *in* versus bandits who were *out* of power. However, no man's friend was every man's enemy, so Juan had to become a past master at outwitting his neighbors when they occasionally joined forces to descend on the ranch exasperatedly seeking his gold and his life—on their part, more irritation than real dislike. Juan was better at that game than they. He told us many stories of his brushes with the enemy, chuckling as if the whole affair were nothing more serious than a friendly game of hide-and-seek. He possessed a few mangy dogs, which he cherished as the rarest of allies, because, as he put it, "Ten men might go to sleep all at the same time, but not one of my dogs ever sleeps."

On one occasion his insomnia-dogs gave him warning of prowlers, whereupon Juan hastily shinned up the water pipe to the roof of the hacienda and lay snugly hidden behind the parapet while searchers ransacked the plantation. When they turned to leave he put a farewell bullet through the crown of the leader's hat, and the orderly retreat straightway became a scrambled Marathon.

On that occasion, as on every other, he smirked under the laurels of victory, and the Piste villagers resigned themselves with extraordinary good nature and profound respect for the only man who could hold his own against them single-handed.

Through Juan word filtered mysteriously over the countryside that workmen were required, and soon the forest paths began to disgorge quantities of strange little Indians who were enticed by the prospect of Mexican silver and even more moved by curiosity as to what the peculiar white man was up to now.

Their attitude toward the old temples was even more disinterested than our own. I never cease to wonder at the detached manner with which they survey the handi-work of their ancestors. They seem to feel not the slightest relationship with old Chichen Itza—being separated by the few hundred years that have elapsed since the breakdown of the Itza power as completely as if the temples and palaces had been erected by the Russians in Siberia. This, even though almost to a man they bear names which the old chronicles record as belonging to the nobles of the ancient city.

A colonnaded hall, abutting one corner of the court, was chosen as ground for our first trial, and the little Indians were set to work with wheelbarrow, pick, and shovel. They were as cheerful a gang as I have ever seen. Chattering and laughing the whole day through, they ate away the mound of dirt industriously as so many ants.

Some of the workers acquired an early dexterity with our civilized tools, and others appeared hopeless in their clumsy fumbling. There is an art even in ditch digging. The next opportunity you get, watch a gang of dirt diggers awhile, and you will see a few who are clever and graceful as tennis players in their movements, and others who painfully batter and prod at the earth—all muscle but sleepy brain; and you will find that the latter accomplish only about half as much as the men who make the job look easy. So it was with our Mayas. Some were quick to learn, some were just plain lazy, and some, no matter how hard they tried, never seemed to get the knack.

Earl circled around like a watchful hawk searching

for just such traits. The lazy ones received short shrift, but be it to the credit of the Maya, such were very few. The habits which had long ago, by brute force and industry, erected artificial stone mountains upon the flattened plain, were evidently not lost. The old genius was gone, but the cheerful stick-to-it-iveness remained in our workmen, making them as delightful to handle as anyone could wish.

They adored practical jokes. The whole crowd of us got a tremendous laugh one day over a trick played on old Jorge Pot, a white-haired joker himself, who had many a score to his credit (Fig. 11). Earl had issued heavy cotton gloves to the wheelbarrowmen to make it possible for them to grip the iron handles which burned under the terrific noonday sun. One forenoon while Jorge was away for a time, one of the diggers unearthed a six-inch scorpion—a wicked and dangerous insect that looks somewhat like a small black lobster and has a poison sting in its long lashing tail, which on some occasions proves deadly and always is painful to a degree. The digger cut off the sting with his shovel, then picked up the now harmless insect and put it in one of old Jorge's gloves which lay on a near-by stump, imprisoning it with a small stone. Soon the iron wheelbarrow handles began to grow uncomfortably hot, so Jorge reached for his gloves, while the rest of us waited breathlessly. As his hand encountered the scorpion he howled and jerked it out, but the sticky claws clung

*(a) The Bandit,
Pablo Tun.*

*(c) Remedios used to
buy "love potions."*

*(b) Old Jorge said, "I
look like a strong
man, so please don't
tell your friends the
barrel is empty."*

*(d) Tarsisio,
our gardener,
watch mender,
barber, tin-
smith, etc.*

*(e) Tuche, the
youngest mem-
ber on the
Carnegie pay-
roll.*

*(f) Pay day taxi service out to the railroad. One sad day the dump truck
dumped in full career, and skinned every elbow in the crowd.*

Fig. 12

WHEN A GRASSHOPPER PLAGUE BROUGHT FAMINE IN ITS WAKE

I played clerk of exchange on pay day, dispensing corn instead of silver.

tightly around his thumb while the now harmless tail lashed furiously again and again at the sensitive bare palm. The poor old man, who had visions of a Pot funeral, leaped in imagined agony and finally, by a tremendous flip, managed to shake off the incubus, which sailed in a neat parabola to land on the neck of the very chap who had started the rumpus. A scorpion is unpleasant, sting or not, and this was very nice retribution indeed. When the unfortunate thing was finally disposed of, a completely demoralized staff and crew leaned weakly against whatever there was handy, heaving chests and streaming eyes bespeaking a capacity for laughter drained to the very dregs.

The fact that in their odd moments some of the crew indulged in a bloodthirsty banditry never interfered with their work at all, nor was a single hand ever raised against us. One and all, they adored "the Engineer," as they called Earl, and I fully believe that if he should decide to turn bandit himself he would be unanimously elected to captaincy of as trained and thoroughgoing a gang of scoundrels as ever took the warpath.

The leaders of the crew are the Tun family, of whom Pablo is the chief. Personally, I am very fond of Pablo, whose picture you will find in Figure 11, and who appeared to be one of the gentlest, most humorous people I have ever seen. Yet, it is reported that not

eight years ago he deemed it necessary to make away
with an enemy who was reputed to be more than
usually intelligent. And they say that Pablo, following
an old Maya custom, devoured the unfortunate man's
brains in order to acquire for himself the benefit of such
an extraordinary intellect. Thus it became a regular
password among the staff whenever we met him to say,
"Pablo Tun, he eats brains," and then everybody would
shout with laughter, including Pablo, who didn't have
the slightest idea what amused us so.

The men were quite intrigued by an ingenious hopper
that Earl rigged up in order to facilitate the removal
of excavated dirt. It was constructed on high stilts so
that the Ford dump trucks could be run beneath to receive the accumulated débris from a box above, which,
when full, was emptied by releasing a trap door in the
bottom (Fig. 13). Long plank runways led to and from
the hopper. Often the wheelbarrowmen, until they
learned the knack, in tipping their barrows to empty
the contents, used to pitch forward with them into the
box. This procedure would occasion great merriment,
as you might imagine, and evidently a good deal of discussion would go on about it in their thatched huts
after work.

One morning I saw a gentleman of Piste who had never
worked for us come weaving up the road. He had evidently been imbibing too freely of "ardent waters"

of Yucatan. Earl watched him talk to a wheelbarrow-man for a moment, then take hold of the handles of the barrow himself and run it up the narrow plank to the hopper. So much he negotiated successfully, but when he dumped it, the usual thing happened. Only this time someone had neglected to close the trap door at the bottom, and the poor fellow tumbled completely through, landing squarely on the top of his head ten feet below. Earl rushed to the rescue, probably already phrasing words of condolence to the sorrowing family. However, our friend picked himself up, though a bit dazed, and when he succeeded in focusing on the Engineer, he bowed low with courtly grace, and grasping Earl's hand, assured him cordially, "It is no fault of yours, my dearest friend, pray do not concern yourself. I have heard stories of this machine, and I find it fully as wonderful as is said. And now I must bid you good-morning."

Another day a fat pig followed his master the long hot three miles from their common dwelling to the Court of the Thousand Columns. It seemed that even the pig was moved by curiosity to leave his slothful home and investigate the untoward happenings at Chichen. When he arrived, he appeared to discover some strange affiliation between himself and the dump truck, because everywhere that dump truck went, the pig was sure to go. Back and forth, from the dumping ground to the dirt hopper, the pig scampered after his new companion with an enthusiasm and persistence worthy of a better cause. Finally the heat and the terrific pace began to tell and he took advantage of the brief halts at the two ends of the line to get forty winks on the side. But as soon as the car started, with an answering grunt he was off after it. As the hours went on, the mechanical perfection of Mr. Ford's handiwork began to triumph over his piggish locomotion, and the poor beast would lose ground until he was completely off schedule. Finally, when the evening bell rang, I believe we were as relieved as the pig, who wearily fell in behind his owner for the long trudge home. We may imagine his mother saying to him, "Why, Piggie dear, how slim you have become!" and his futile explanations of the wonders of the great outside world to a narrow-minded and untraveled elder generation.

CHAPTER IX

Rebuilding Stone Serpents at the Temple Door

T HE first season at Chichen Itza, short as it was, well fulfilled our desire. We knew now what we were up against. A beginning at actual excavation had been made, giving the feel of the matter, the major domo had proved eminently satisfactory, workmen had been broken in, and future requirements of staff and equipment had become clearer.

The next January, 1925, found us back again doubled in numbers, and accompanied by solid carloads of food, furniture, autos, and machinery. The trucks were assembled at the railway station and for two weeks these cars plied back and forth, hauling in the supplies. We were working against time, for Dr. Merriam, the president of the Carnegie Institution of Washington, was due in a month to make us a visit. As I said before, the Carnegie Institution was responsible for the work at Chichen Itza, hence Dr. Merriam was particularly interested in the findings of his new project. With him were coming Dr. Clark Wissler of the American Museum of Natural History of New York and Dr. A. V. Kidder, chairman of the National Research Council.

With such a distinguished audience in prospect we felt spurred to prodigies of labor in order to do justice to Chichen in the short time allowed. Two major lines of activity were immediately gotten under way. One was the establishment of satisfactory living quarters, and the other was the continuance of the previous season's work on the Court of the Thousand Columns. We already had to our credit a large colonnaded hall in which a carved stone altar held the central place. But after the experience so acquired, Earl and Dr. Morley were ambitious to tackle a bigger job.

An enormous tree-crested mound, which stood adjacent to the northwest corner of the court, had drawn Earl's attention the year before. It was an unprepossessing shapeless lump of earth which appeared to have little but size to recommend it, but time and again I would see Earl drifting in its direction, clambering its steep slopes, measuring and scribbling notes, all with an attitude half-dubious, half-excited. I followed him one day to the crest and found him staring straight down into the mound, as if he might divine what secret the great thing had hidden in its heart. (Fig. 1)

"What about it, Earl?" I asked.

"I don't know—hunch, I guess," he answered, "because it doesn't look like anything but quantity, does it?"

A few more days of hesitation, then Juan received his orders: "Clear the mound of bush. Work begins Monday morning." Then, as an afterthought, "Leave the bigger trees—I think we will find them useful." It perhaps was fortunate that at that time Earl did not realize the almost impossible intricacies and problems which that harmless-looking heap sheltered in its heart. If he had known he might have quailed before the complex of buildings piled upon buildings, pyramids within pyramids, hidden paintings, grotesque sculpture, buried sacrificial treasure, and tunneled passages which were not to be completely unfolded until four years of concentrated work had been devoted to the task.

But at the end of that time, the drab and tumbled mountain of earth and broken stone had been transformed into the magnificent gleaming-white Temple of the Warriors, a monument to archeological devotion and skill unsurpassed anywhere in the entire world.

When the obscuring undergrowth had been removed the contours of the mound revealed themselves more clearly. It flanked the Court of the Columns on its southern side, appearing attached to the long range of columns there, while the east and west slopes fell precipitately fifty feet to the ground level. But on the west, or front, a series of three great stair-like steps gave variety to the profile.

You will notice on the photograph (Fig. 40) that the western range of the court (that hall, by the way, called the Whispering Gallery by the talkative painter in the fantasy of Chapter VII) extends entirely across the front and somewhat beyond the Temple of the Warriors. In its ruined state this long mound stood about twelve feet high and fifty broad, providing the first great stair step I mentioned in the profile. Along the part where it adjoins the temple, the structure is named the Northwest Colonnade.

From this platform, which was twelve feet high, the sides of the mound sloped abruptly upward, although in the center a ramp less steep ran to a height of about three fourths the pyramid's altitude. At this point

Fig. 13   *Courtesy of Carnegie Institution*

Earl and Gustav rigged up a hopper with long plank runways from temple to Ford truck to help the wheelbarrow men dispose of their loads.

Fig. 14   *Courtesy of Carnegie Institution*

The Temple of the Warriors, during the process of excavation and repair.

Fig. 15

TEMPLE OF THE WARRIORS

Looking through the great front door toward the Altar of Sacrifice. The Plumed Serpent, a horrible Maya god with vicious fangs and sinuous feathered body, was stylized in stone into door pillars.

both ramp and slope flattened out a second time on to another level terrace. It would seem that the ramp represented the ruins of a staircase and that the second flat terrace was the top of the pyramid. Therefore, the tumbled heap of débris, about sixty feet square, which rose some fourteen feet above the terrace, providing the third setback above mentioned, was the temple itself, for which the huge pyramidal base had been provided.

A search for surface indications revealed the tops of square columns at the very crest of the mound— columns that must have been an essential part of temple structure itself. The same kind of square columns cropped up from the mold along the whole length of the Northwest Colonnade. Moreover, on the platform at the top of the staircase lay a reclining human figure, headless and pitted by the storms of centuries. Near by, and half buried in the débris, were found two huge blocks of stone carved in the form of rattlesnake tails. These curious features we recognized immediately, as there were many others of the same kind in Chichen Itza. They had formed the tops of two serpent columns which at one time flanked the great front doorway (see Fig. 15).

The serpent column is one of the weirdest, most bizarre architectural features in the world. It represents the Plumed Serpent, who was the chief god of Chichen

Itza. His form has no counterpart in reality, for Nature, in all of her eccentric creations, overlooked the grotesque and terrible combination of a great serpent covered with the feathers of a bird. But the queer dark Maya brain evolved the horrible creature, creating a god which was beyond human experience, and which coiled so tightly around the natural life of man as almost to strangle him through fear of it.

His image is painted and carved upon temple walls, hundreds of times repeating gaping fanged jaws and feather-covered slimy curves. But when used as a supporting column, the body is stiffened into a heavy upright to hold the lintels over the door—a device conforming to a practical architectural necessity, and at the same time representing the god-horror to whom the temple was dedicated.

As you will see in the illustration of one of these columns (Fig. 15), the head with wide-flung jaws, vicious fangs, and long tongue lies flat upon the platform. Behind it the body rises stiffly and vertically as a column shaft. Then at its crest it turns abruptly forward for a few feet to provide a base for the wooden lintels over the door and finally bends again straight upward in plume-tufted rattles of stone a hundred times more massive than those of the deadly rattlesnake himself.

The whole of it was painted from fang to rattle tip in colors half natural and half mystic. The inside of the mouth was a deep red, the fangs white, the lips yellow, while the eye reversed the usual coloring, having a white pupil set in a socket of black paste. The feathers of the body and those forming the tuft at the tip of the rattles were green, the rattles themselves were blue, while the scales on the creature's unfeathered belly were yellow.

Color, carving, and position follow a rigid and set pattern with little difference in all of its occurrences. Therefore, when the two stone tails were found upon the temple platform, Earl knew instantly not only what he would find, but where to look. He set one group of his men at work with pick and shovel upon the outer edge of the pyramid platform where the débris was shallow. In a short time they reached a plaster floor, beautifully polished, and colored red. Then the work progressed inward toward the great front door. As they drew slowly nearer, Earl and I became as excited as cats who watch a mouse hole, but I fear we lacked that animal's still patience. We were terribly afraid that when the temple roof collapsed the tons of stone had crashed on the serpent heads, reducing them to powder.

Then at last a shout from Juan: "*La piedra grande.*"

"The great stone," echoed Earl, as he seized a pick from a workman's hands and cautiously cleared débris first from one great painted head, then from the other.

They were in perfect condition. The greatest good luck in the world had played into our hands, for it became clear that instead of the roof collapsing suddenly on top of the precious objects, the topmost walls had crumbled slowly while the rains had washed down plaster and mortar and small rubble, until the heads were entirely buried. So when the lintels broke and the great crash came, the protective cushion of débris took the shock, and the serpent heads lay perfectly preserved throughout the long waiting centuries. (Figs. 16 and 17.)

The shaft blocks which made up the bodies had toppled forward and lay one before the other in almost perfect alignment. The problem at hand, then, was to put back these blocks, so the diggers were transferred elsewhere. By this time they had cleared the platform to the front wall of the temple and had penetrated through the open doorway to a point shortly behind the first block of the serpent shaft, which had remained in its original position. This left a straight cut bank twelve feet high at the temple door and its top would serve admirably as a base from which to work in lifting the column blocks into position.

I am going to describe the setting up of these serpent columns in some detail, because the procedure so excellently typifies the kind of problem that is continually and unexpectedly cropping up in the field archeologist's life. One day never knows what the next day will bring forth, and hence it is an absolute impossibility to provide for all emergencies when outfitting for an expedition. Then, when actually in the field, one is as cut off from shops and last-minute necessities as was Robinson Crusoe on his island. Wit and ingenuity are the only means of solution. A man must provide for all his needs with the odds and ends that accumulate in his pockets or from the treasures of the junkroom. Even the garbage can, on occasion, provides its quota of incalculable value. I have seen keys made out of copper pennies, automobile bearings replaced with very efficient bacon rind, stovepipe rigged from tomato cans, torn shoes resoled with auto tires, and aching teeth filled with plaster-of-Paris and crockery cement.

In the business of replacing the serpent columns, the trees left uncut were of enormous value as anchor posts for brace ropes. Their myriad live roots gave them such a clutch upon the earth as could never be equaled by posts wedged in man-dug pits. Rope and fresh-cut timbers were accumulated. The latter was easily procured from the all-surrounding forest, while as for the former, it is the chief product of the great sisal plantations of the peninsula. The world's greatest source of sisal rope lay at our very door. Grant the Maya Indian enough rope and he can do almost anything. It was with timber and rope and sheer man power that the great stone structures which we were excavating had been built so long ago.

As the operations on the two columns were identical, I will describe but one. The first step involved the setting up of a great rope-lashed timber form, somewhat like a grotesque capital A, between the back of the column and the twelve-foot dirt bank. It stood four feet higher than would the top of the finished column and was braced by guy ropes to the trees. In the crotch at its tip the butt of a hardwood tree trunk forty feet long was laid horizontally so that its farther end rested far back on the top of the mound—an adequate counter-balance for anything less than a ton in weight. Then a powerful chain block and tackle was securely lashed to the butt, where it overhung the serpent head sixteen feet below. Thus was improvised a hoist which proved adequate to all demands.

One by one the square-cut stone blocks making up the segments of the upright serpent body were gripped by rope handles and hoisted into place. They were wedged with tiny spalls of stone, and the cracks between blocks were completely sealed with a mud shell except for a small hole into which a pipe was thrust. Through this, liquid cement was forced, which bound the blocks to one another so tightly as to make of the ever-heightening shaft a single solid stone. These blocks only weighed from 400 to 700 pounds and hence were easily raised.

However, the capital of the column, that right-angled stone cut to represent serpent rattles and flowing plumes, which was to cap the whole, was a far more complicated proposition. To begin with, it weighed well over a ton, but that was not the chief difficulty. As you will see in the illustration (Fig. 18) this final block looks distinctly top-heavy. The center of gravity lies out in space over the serpent's head, and it seemed impossible to keep it in place without unsightly supports from below. Originally the stone had been held in position by the tremendous weight of the temple façade and roof which rested on its tenon, which in turn bore directly upon the column shaft. But as Earl had no intention of ever restoring the roof of the building, some other scheme had to be devised to anchor the thousands of pounds of stone so securely that it would never crash down upon the carven heads below.

First it was moved on wooden rollers to a position beside the column. It was wrapped with heavy rope and hooked on to the chain tackle. And then, to a rhythmic chant of the men pulling on the tackle, the chain gradually shortened, but the block rose not at all. Consternation reigned for a moment, till Earl ascertained that the forty-foot counterbalance of timber, long and ponderous as it was, had proved unequal to the enormous weight of stone and at its far end was describing a skyward arc. This was soon remedied by making use of the entire mass of our visitors, and we had many, for half the countryside was agog over the proceedings. They were politely but firmly requested to sit along the whole forty-foot length and not to move under any conceivable circumstance. The added two tons of Maya flesh and bone proved more than adequate, and the heavy stone rose slowly until it was precariously poised over the column. Then the chains were slackened a bit till it rested on its base, and the counterbalance was securely lashed down to one of the trees. Anxiously Earl inspected the balance and each of the ropes, for if anything at all should give or break, the beautiful serpent head below was doomed.

So far all was safe, but the procedure from here on required ingenuity and skill that would not permit a single error. There was a bar of tool steel in the stores, and on our forge it was beaten and tempered into the shape of a miner's drill. Then Karl Ruppert, who was Earl's assistant and knew the handling of a churn drill, all the next day led a gang of four men who stood on a scaffold above the poised column lifting and driving the drill straight down into the shaft. Deeper and deeper it penetrated through tail and column, even into the ground underneath. Then a long slim bar of soft iron was threaded at one end while the other was split to permit the introduction of an iron wedge. This end, wedge and all, was lowered through the bore until it touched the earth. Heavy hammer blows from above drove the wedge at the bottom farther in, splitting the iron and spreading it to the full diameter of the bore. After this liquid cement was slowly poured in, until it

Fig. 16

*Tumbled débris on the front platform of the Warriors, from which the
elements of the great Plumed Serpent columns were recovered.*

Fig. 17

*Portrait of the Plumed Serpent, which was brilliantly painted in colors
half natural, half mystic.*

Fig. 18

ANCHORING THE SERPENT TAIL IN PLACE

The process of raising and securing this unwieldy block, weighing well over a ton, excellently illustrates archeological ingenuity.

overflowed at the top, and we knew that when it had set, that which had been a continuous hole would become a rigid bar which would tie the whole column to the foundation beneath.

As a final touch, a slot was cut around the tip of the rod, a steel plate was fitted over its threaded top, and a heavy nut was drawn tight. This was then covered with cement, so that not a single trace remained of the fourteen-foot bolt which united capital, shaft, and foundation into a solid unified substance.

When after some days the tackle was removed, the column stood firm and steady, a triumph to archeological imagination and engineering skill—the first great step toward the final goal.

CHAPTER X

Finding the Altar of Sacrifice

AFTER the erection of the two serpent columns, our diggers felt a great relief at not having to work under those shafts of toppling stone, so they fell like busy moles upon the interior of the temple. They found rows of columns and bounding walls that stood all the way from two feet in height to the full twelve feet as they were when built. Across the interior of the temple a partition wall was uncovered, with a narrow door in its center which led to an interior room.

This appeared to be the Inner Sanctuary so common to Maya temples, and therein Earl knew he ought to find the Altar of Sacrifice. So he abandoned the steady forward march for a moment and set the diggers to sinking pits in the sanctuary against the back wall. True enough, the altar was there, a great table of stone originally measuring nine by thirteen feet, but smashed by the collapse of the roof into many fragments (Fig. 19). Patient work plus the hawklike eyes of old Juan located every splinter of the stone tablets making up the table tops, and eventually they were put together so skillfully that the surface lay smooth and flat as it had so long ago.

Fortunately the supports of these stones were unharmed, and they are probably the queerest sort of table legs to be found in the world. Nineteen little stone human beings holding their hands upward served the purpose. They are splendidly carved little chaps, strong and smooth, with faces so different from each other that surely they are portraits of actual human beings who one time took part in the old city's life (Fig. 20).

One can well imagine a sculptor crouched in front of one of the statues roughly blocking out its general contours, then hailing a passing friend: "Hi there, old man, wait a minute—I want to do your picture. There now, face the light. That's right. Now raise your fists beside your ears, and quit grinning. This is serious."

When the carving was finished, the little figures were painted in gaudy colors from tip to toe. Their skin was colored red or brown, and some of the faces were wildly slashed across with white and black lines. The old Mayas often did this; they thought it made them more terrifying in battle. It certainly had a startling effect upon their features as we found them.

One thing was very peculiar. The altar had stood about three feet high, and every single one of these little stone men measured three feet and nine inches. The extra nine inches was buried in the temple floor, and since this covered them to about the mid-shins, tiny clay feet had been molded and fitted straight in front of their legs. At first we thought somebody had made a mistake in calculation, and were amused to imagine a scene between an angry architect and repentant sculptors who, in an effort to appease, dug their statues down into the floor and then, in a panic, molded stucco feet to make them look "just as good." However, two years later, an accidental comparison of some measurements threw a sudden bright light on the whole matter. But what it was belongs not to this chapter. Another story will have to be told in completeness before the explanation will fully explain.

Probably one of the most interesting features of this altar—certainly the most gruesome—lay in a small detail which we almost overlooked in those hot sunlit days of excavation. The top of the altar and the sanctuary floor were painted red. A small thing that seems, doesn't it? But think first what the word *altar* means. It implies sacrifice, and sacrifice, to the Maya, meant the slaughtering of a human being. Picture to yourself the poor victim stretched out on his back in a dim torch-lit room, with ankles and wrists firmly clutched by temple attendants. The High Priest paces slowly toward him, knife in hand, while prayers are chanted by the onlookers in guttural excited tempo. A pause of dead quiet except for the captive's moans—a shriek as the knife plunges—then hellish pandemonium breaks loose, while the dripping, still-struggling heart is torn out and lifted high and triumphantly in the air. Blood spurts wildly, then drips slowly and soaks deep into an already blood-dyed altar and floor. A dreadful and sickening sight! No wonder that *the altar was painted red so the bloodstains wouldn't show.*

Very dreadful things rarely happen in the clean bright heat of sunlight. When man plans deeds of horror he chooses the covering mystery of night and darkness. This Inner Sanctuary where stood the Altar of Sacrifice was originally shrouded in perpetual gloom. No windows pierced the thick stone walls. The roof rose in lines of narrow vaults full twenty-five feet into turgid, smoky darkness. The single low narrow door was covered with a thick woven curtain, while the divisions of the outer portal themselves were hung with tapestries of heavy stuff which shut out the least ray of the sun. A dim smoky torch or two and the smoldering bowls of incense provided all the light there was. When we remember all this, the blood-stenched Chamber of Sacrifice becomes a place of creeping horror which it is difficult now to visualize.

To-day the sanctuary stands open to the light. Cold clean rains have swept the altar free from its matting of bloody filth, for the roof has gone. It fell centuries ago, probably during those days when the coming of the white man so disturbed America. Its riven bulk crashed into the temple beneath, filling the walls to fullness and grinding everything beneath its fall.

Maya roofs were ponderous and wonderful things. They were constructed in the form of high vaults which rested upon the outer walls and upon wooden beams stretching from column to column. The roof stones were cut with a long tail which stretched back into solid masonry. Each row as it was placed upon the one beneath jutted forward slightly, and heavy stone weights were placed upon the tail to hold it down. Thus the two sides of the arch gradually converged toward each other until they lacked only one foot of meeting. At this stage the top gap was covered by flat capstones and the vault was complete. You can see that the strength of the roof lay in its great weight, for the only thing to hold the in-leaning blocks in place was the ever-increasing solid masonry piled upon their ends. But although this was its strength, at the same time it was its greatest danger. For, as I said before, this tremendous weight rested ultimately upon wooden beams, which spanned the distance between the column supports. These beams were the weakest point of construction, for in a damp climate wood will rot, and rotten wood is a sorry support for a thousand tons of stone.

Maya roofs were constructed in a manner different from any other that the world has seen. The Maya never learned to brace shaped blocks against a "keystone" at the peak of a vault. They thought by sheer bulk to attain the end which the principle of the true arch so perfectly achieves. The true arch was discovered in the Tigris-Euphrates Valley, more than five thousand years ago, thence spread all over the Old World, but was never hit upon in the New.

In so many ways the natives of this continent just missed the great fundamental ideas which made civilization easy. They never thought to domesticate animals, so they never had milk or a constant supply of meat; and at the same time they missed the speed of travel possible to a horse, and their tired backs carried the loads that should have belonged to the burro. They never thought of a wheel, so they had to drag by main force the enor-

mous loads of stone and other goods which it was necessary to transport. They never found out how to employ
iron and brass for cutting tools, and so had to hack and
chip out their magnificent architecture and sculpture
by using stone on stone. The time involved must have
been infinitely great. In every way, their lives were
slower, harder, and more painful. And for that very
reason we must give them greater honor for the unend-
ing patience, brutal toil, and sheer grit which went into
the great works they performed.

The wood used for the temple beams usually was from
a tree called *sapote*, the sap of which provides the base
for our modern chewing gum. The trees of Yucatan are
not at all like those we know—their names are different
and their characteristics are usually very surprising.
It seems as if everything in the tropics is just a little bit
more violent than customary. The people certainly are;
the snakes are more deadly; the insects are more vicious;
and even the trees, while they have few dangerous qualities, seem to have an exaggerated sort of character.

Now these sapote beams, for instance, are noted for
terrifically long life. They are very slow to decay, even
in an almost perpetual tropic damp, and some of those
timbers that were hoisted into place a thousand years
ago are still sturdily supporting ponderous Maya stone
temple roofs as securely as when they were new. If the
architect of the Temple of the Warriors had not been

Fig. 19

THE TEMPLE ALTAR

*Smashed to bits by the falling roof. Maya ceremonials dealt largely
with bloody human sacrifice, enacted on such tables of polished stone.*

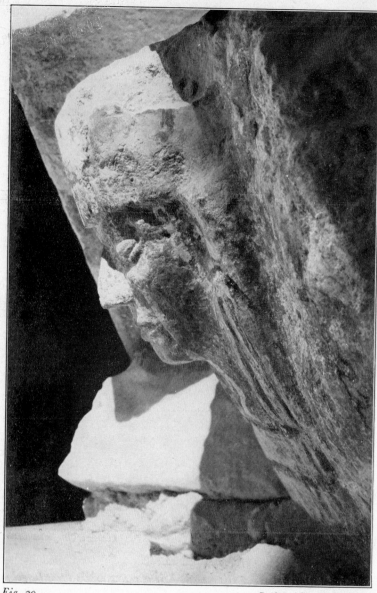

Fig. 20

Courtesy of Carnegie Institution

A MAYA PORTRAIT IN STONE
One of the human statuettes from the Atlantean Altar.

just a bit too ambitious, his structure too would be standing to-day as solid as it seemed upon the day it was completed. But he used far too many wooden beams and too few stone supports, and he planned that their span should be too great. Some of his columns stood thirteen feet apart, and the bridging of this thirteen-foot gap was too great a strain for even the famous "wood of iron."

But if the sapote has been called the wood of iron, there is another tree in the jungle, named *cholul*, which deserves the name of the "wood of tempered steel." Earl made its surprising acquaintance one day early in his first year in Yucatan. He was setting up an anvil which he had brought from the United States for the purpose of sharpening the men's tools. He needed some sort of foundation on which to rest it, so he ordered the major domo to send a couple of woodcutters to get him a short log of hard wood.

"Hard wood, Engineer?"

"Yes, very hard wood, Juan," unsuspectingly answered Earl, who had been brought up in the moderate, civilized forests of the United States.

The whole day passed, and no wood appeared, which was exasperating. I remember that Earl asked Juan's son if he had gone to Spain to get it and wasn't much comforted to get the invariable answer, "*Quién sabe?*" ("Who knows?")

But the afternoon of the following day a solemn procession turned in at the hacienda gate, and with measured tread approached, bearing a stumpy little log not seven feet long cradled on bars across their shoulders. Eight men strong they were, and we who were lounging comfortably around the tea table indulged in a few remarks about two days' wages for eight men, with nothing but a small chunk of wood to show.

"Square the end of that, Juan, and then we'll set it up." So the great cross-cut saw was brought, and two men set to work.

"Oh, Engineer, the saw doesn't cut," the plaintive cry arose.

"A brand-new saw ought to cut," said Earl, and he went down to investigate. The teeth looked all right, so Earl handed it back to them with a few well-chosen remarks about the relation between their wages and a good day's work. But this time he stood watching them. The saw certainly wasn't getting anywhere at all. So he grabbed one end and laid his own strong back to the task. The saw slid around as if it were riding on smooth hard bone, and then for the first time he looked at his wood carefully. He attempted to lift one end; it was as if anchored to the ground. He tried his pocket knife on an edge and the blade turned like cheese. Then he looked reproachfully at Juan, who, I regret to say, twinkled a bit maliciously as he remarked: "But you ordered very hard wood, Engineer."

Finally, however, some sort of smooth surface was

achieved, and then about five feet of the log was buried in the ground to hold it firm, and the anvil was hoisted to its top. But now another problem came up. For the anvil had to be anchored to its base. Earl thought he knew his wood by this time, so he procured four long spikes and a sledge hammer. The first spike was tapped in till it stood by itself, then with a great swing the sledge crashed down. But the spike which couldn't possibly penetrate the close fibers of the cholul, glanced from the head of the hammer and went singing like a bullet over the top of the tallest tree in the courtyard. When this had happened a few times, a good bit of head scratching ensued. Earl doesn't let anything baffle him for long—so he finally fixed it up all shipshape by boring a hole horizontally clear through his stubborn log and lashing the anvil down with heavy wire. Finally the job was done, tempers were frayed, almost every tool on the plantation was tattered and dulled, but our education on Yucatan wood had advanced several lessons.

Later we discovered a twin to the cholul which is called *quebra acha* or "ax breaker." It can't possibly be cut unless the ax or machete blades are first smeared with a juice of another tree—then everything proceeds merrily.

There is the *yaxec*, a yellow wood with a stinging sap, one drop of which is enough to blind a person for life, and other trees with a sap, blood-red in color, which makes a stain that never comes out.

And there is the *jabin*, which when once it starts to burn never goes out. This is very useful to the Maya housewife who lives far from the supply of matches, for when she leaves home for a few days she sets one end of the long tree trunk in her burning hearth and lets the rest trail out of the door. The fire eats slowly and steadily down the stick, and is ready and waiting to provide hot coals for a fresh hearth when the family come home.

Among the plants most useful to the Maya are the *bahucas*. They are long trailing vines which hang from the treetops to the ground in a thick tangle of streamers throughout the forest. When water-soaked, they are strong and pliant as rope, and are used for everything under the sun, but particularly to tie together the wooden framework of the thatched roofs (Figs. 21 and 22). A house without a nail in it is characteristic of Yucatan, and it is the useful *bahuca* which makes this possible. A tied-together roof is a far better construction for high winds, because it will give to the gale, where a stiff nailed structure would be ripped to pieces in no time at all.

These are but a few of the outstanding facts that the Maya Indian to-day knows about his country. All of this lore has come down to him through the ages, from father to son, in an unbroken chain which extends for centuries and millenniums back into the dim past of old unknown America.

Medicines from plants; foodstuffs from wild animals and birds and reptiles as well as from the soil and the sea; dyes from shells and trees and earths; wood and palm for houses; lime and stone for temples; clays for pottery; reeds for baskets, wild fruits, gaudy feathers, homemade cloth and shoes, precious stones and metals —all these lie ready for the taking, for him who knows where to search.

When a people live on the land, and from the land, far from great markets and stores and factories; when their very life depends on what they can gather from raw Nature with their bare hands—it behooves them to study and to know what their land can give.

CHAPTER XI

Field Headquarters

W E SET up housekeeping our first year in a rather primitive manner. The big hacienda house and all of the smaller outlying buildings had been rented by the Carnegie Institution, but they were in wretched repair and so we fitted ourselves into a few reasonably dry and shady quarters wherever we could find them.

Jerry Kilmartin had taken a small palm-thatched hut as his house, while he made a survey map of the old city, and during the long months of revolution, while he was cut off from mail and was awaiting our coming, had entertained armies from both sides with strict and apprehensive impartiality. He had become so cautious in expressing his political views that even when peace prevailed again and we, his friends, appeared on the scene, we couldn't extract any details from him about his experiences except that the Mexicans were "all right" and that he guessed he knew the text of the one English book he had with him by heart, and that this idea of taking one book to be wrecked with on a desert island didn't provide at all adequately against monotony.

Our arrival was a great day for Jerry, and he provided a noble feast with which to celebrate. Menu cards were written after the best traditions, and we all signed them as a memento of our first meal in Chichen Itza. A dining room and kitchen was set up on Jerry's mud-floored front porch, and when the rainy season broke, the kitchen end was often flooded a foot deep by a gushing torrent. I can remember seeing old Jimmy, the cook, wading up to his shins as he pottered about the single little charcoal brazier where he concocted the delicious four-course meals which he provided us.

Jimmy was a Chinaman who had worked half his life

for Americans in Yucatan, and prided himself on his English. I'll never forget how astonished I was to find out that Chinamen really did say "Me catchee de wash" on laundry day, and I used to take great glee in ordering fried rice just to hear Jimmy repeat after me, "Flied lice?" He told us the cheerful tale of one place where he had worked, where the family was particularly fond of one of his soups. One day when the mistress of the house was investigating kitchen affairs, the savory concoction was bubbling on the stove. She poked a fork into it and was horror-stricken to fish out a boiled rat. "Oh, it's all lite," said Jimmy blandly. "The lat's for me, the soup for you!" To this day when Earl says to me, "You like maybe cup-coffee?" I reply according to ritual, "No, I like lat-soup."

Dr. Morley, Jerry, and Munroe bunked in Jerry's hut, and while a little house was being built for Earl and myself across the yard, we took a room in the old historic hacienda building. Almost immediately we were to learn how really precarious tropic existence is, and how constantly care must be exercised. I remember the first morning when I awoke, I peered out from my mosquito-net canopy straight into the staring eyes of a brown snake that was sitting on the window sill. Earl says I announced with some indignation, "There's a snake *looking* at me," quite as if the phenomenon of snakes in my bedroom was to be expected, so long as they were discreet about it. Then he says I added reassuringly, "But it's a very small snake." I had been present the day before at the finding of a boa constrictor among the banana trees, so I was entirely erroneously basing my emotions on the size of the reptile. A couple of years later, I was clearing out the cobwebs from our shoe box after six months in the States, and, finding the accumulation too thick for effective work with a wet rag, I took the box outside and turned it upside down, spilling out a coral snake which had been under one of the shelves. Small as it is, the *coralea* is probably the most dangerous snake in America, as there is no antidote for its poison, and a single drop of the venom inflicts a horrible death within a few minutes. When I realized that my bare hand had come within an ace of touching it several times, I literally grew icy cold and began to shake with great convulsive shudders in a reaction of terror and relief.

Perhaps it wouldn't be out of place here to tell about those early days when I was caught off my guard and was thoroughly stung by a scorpion. The scorpion is a vicious-looking red or black insect somewhat resembling a small crab, having a long jointed tail fixed with a stinger in its tip. The beast is extraordinarily cranky and lashes out with this stinger at the slightest provocation. Some types are deadly, but those in Yucatan are fatal only to children. However, their poison affects the various nerve centers and results in extreme discomfort.

The first law of the jungle, for human beings at least, is *never* to put your hand in a place where you can't see. Snakes, scorpions, centipedes, tarantulas—all lurk in dark and hidden corners, with poison fangs set on hair triggers, and a person is foolish indeed who needlessly runs any risk of encounter. I have learned the lesson so well by this time that, no matter where I am, nothing will induce me to slip my hand under a cushion or to grub around in a dark closet, while I have been known to shake my shoes automatically after a night's sleep on the top floor of a brand-new Statler hotel!

One evening after dinner I noticed that the skies seemed to be preparing a particularly beautiful sunset. Clouds, high-banked, were soaked in dyes of Oriental hue, and from near the horizon, long streamers of golden light shot to the zenith. I searched swiftly for a vantage point from which to view it better, for the hacienda lay low among thick trees. My eyes fell on the crest of the Monjas—that majestic ancient palace—which lay not more than three hundred yards away. I set off on a dead run in order to miss as little as possible of the beautiful shifting color playing above my head. Arrived at the foot of the slippery, ruinous, ladder-like stairway, I started up on all fours, padding hand over hand in my haste, much as would a dog, thus placing my hands on each succes- sive step above the level of my eye. I ran a foolish risk, for at the very crest a crackle of living fire seemed to run from a finger tip the whole length of my arm. I pulled myself up just in time to see a grotesque scorpion scuttling for cover.

The tip of my finger pained horribly. The sunset was forgotten as I paced back and forth on the terrace, shaking it in both terror and agony, trying desperately to recall what I had heard about the effect of such a sting. I could remember vaguely that the poison was supposed to affect the nervous system, so I didn't dare try to negotiate those dangerous steps if my powers of locomotion were due to go back on me at any minute. I never felt so isolated and lonely in my life, for I was too far away for a shout to carry, and nobody had seen me start in that direction.

It was a bad few minutes, till I heard the blessed sound of voices, and looking down saw Earl and his foreman seat themselves on the lowest step for a chat. My courage ebbed back with the knowledge of human companionship, so very slowly I started down the steps, and sat down beside them. With an excess of bravado, I said nothing, till Earl happened to look at me.

"What on earth is the matter, Ann?"

But at that precise moment the poison got to my nerve centers. I started to sob helplessly, and through a rapidly thickening tongue I managed to explain. Earl wanted to get me home at once. However, the motor incoördination I had feared above now gripped me so that my knees had no strength and the back of my neck no rigidity. He had to pick me up bodily and lug me back. Except for a persisting difficulty of speech and stinging finger tip, the ill effects lasted but a short time. It had been an ugly dilemma, and I was well out of it.

The building of our little house was an interesting process to follow (Figs. 21 and 22). We had decided to make the architecture of the lesser buildings conform to the style of the country. In earliest Maya times the better houses had been built of lime-plastered stone walls and roofed with a sloping gable of thatch. There were many pictures of them painted on temple walls. The technique has persisted in Yucatan to this day, and we decided to make our house similar, in outward appearance at least. Inside, we installed modern plumbing and finished the floor with cement, dividing the space with partitions into three rooms.

On one matter I was firm. There was a nice little fruit-bearing lemon tree on the house site, so I had the workmen save it, and leave a hole in the floor through which it was to grow and be watered. The plan worked beautifully, and for two years the little tree in our parlor sturdily provided us with lemonade and flavoring for our tea, until the lack of sun proved too much for even its tropic vitality.

As you can see from the illustration, the construction of the roof was a complicated matter. Not a nail was used. The bony framework was raised from the tops of the walls, dependent for anchorage on gravity alone, and was tied together with long pliant *lianas*. The thatch was woven into this, producing a thick water-tight protection, which unfortunately harbored an infinity of wild life of the crawling, creeping variety. We came to regard it as not at all unusual to have things fall around, near, or even on us, but the condition made for scrupulous tucking in of the mosquito canopy as a safeguard at night. During the wet season, the quantity increased almost miraculously, and what had been intermittent plops became as a steady gentle rain upon the place beneath. We wore our hats in the house then.

There were too many thicknesses of the overlapping thatch to make it worth while ever to attempt to clean out the insects, but one year an invading army suddenly visited us and did the job most effectively. Not an army of revolutionists this time; they were ants on the move, migrating for some unknown reason from somewhere to somewhere else, and our house lay in their path. The first we knew, the walls were aswarm and we tried to fight them back with cans of water and sprays of insecticide. But by the thousands they came relentlessly on, and just as we were giving up the battle, old Juan appeared on the scene. "Leave them, Engineer, they will clean your house for you." And so we did, migrating ourselves, and evacuating the premises to the invading hordes. All that day and night they passed and till the next forenoon—a solid column a hundred and fifty feet broad—truly the most prodigious quantity of living things I have ever seen!

The luckless insects which happened to be in their path spread in a panic in all directions, and it was amusing to watch a flock of black birds following on either side of the column and reaping a rich harvest from among the refugees.

The next day our house was clean, even as Juan had predicted. Not a single insect pest survived, although the floor was littered with their mangled remains—too-tough legs and hard shelly backs.

Some of our wild visitors were more permanent in their attentions. There was a great fat toad which every evening just after we had turned on the lights appeared in the doorway and surveyed the floor for succulent bugs. He treated us with more disregard than we did him, for he shot around unconcernedly—a rather logy projectile about six inches square. Self-possession almost always is rewarded, and we made it the business of our lives to procure the very finest meal possible for him. We grew to be very fond of him, naming him Toad-avía after a nebulous Spanish word which means *soon, still, not yet*. He was perfectly omnivorous, gobbling absolutely anything that moved in front of him. I am afraid sometimes we abused his confidence, for occasionally we fed him horny beetles on a string, pulling them back to make him swallow the same one several times. They must have scratched his poor throat badly, and he would bat with his webby little hands at the string of which he couldn't rid his lips. Once we gave him fifteen grains of aspirin and ten of quinine without doing him any visible harm, and on one occasion I offered him a glass flashlight globe which he gulped down like a gentleman. Unfortunately he had a host of relatives who frequented a pot hole of rain water in our backyard, and the croakings and bellowings and shriekings that rent the night were almost unbearable, till Earl filled the trysting place with earth.

I had the good fortune actually to see an "armadillo dillowing in his armor," one day when I investigated an inordinate scuffling among the vines near my porch. Never having encountered one before except in the form of a basket, it was quite amusing to watch him on the move. However, a stray dog saw him too and attacked him under my very eyes, so I had to effect a rescue, then I took Mr. Dillo far out into the bush where I thought he'd be safe. But the next day there were more scufflings and I saw that he was back. Again I picked him up and took him out, farther this time, and the next day once more found him back. I never could figure what attraction the vines held, but I was determined I wasn't going to see him murdered in my own yard, so I tucked him under my arm and walked a good two miles along a little-frequented path and set him down with a few well-chosen words of advice which must have taken effect, for I never saw him again.

A great hailstorm that burst on us one April day netted us two more creatures for the menagerie. One was a rabbit which must have been severely injured about the head, because he allowed us to catch him with our hands and stayed quite contentedly around the porch. The other was an adorable faun whose mother had been killed, and when a native brought him in, I fell in love at first sight. I fed him warm milk out of a bottle, and he grew so affectionate he was almost a nuisance. He was under our feet every minute and followed like Mary's Little Lamb. It was impossible even to take a shower without the faun's getting sprayed also. He was such a darling that it almost broke my heart when he sickened and died.

During our second year, when we had had more time for putting our work on a permanent basis, the hacienda house became the center of affairs (Fig. 23). The great *sala* served as a dining room, except when the weather was fine, when we ate out of doors on the corridor. This sala, with which every Spanish building is equipped as a matter of course, is a survival of the great hall of European castle days. It was very big and high and full of echoes, so that when the large staff that gathered in later years was all seated, the place was a veritable madhouse for thrice-repeated din. To converse with anyone except one's own immediate neighbor was an impossibility unless you rose in your place and hallooed at the person you wanted. Ordinary table chit-chat degenerated into a brawl wherein the general tenor of conversation was reduced to shouting, "Did you say *better* or *butter?*" No doubt it was fine for the digestion, but it was hard on the nervous system.

At first we had Maya house boys, but after the bright one went quite mad and the stupid one proved not too dull to loot us right and left, we confined ourselves to China boys.

Alphonso Canton came on as cook after Jimmy had proved unavailable. He was a gentle-souled chap from Merida's Chinatown, and could cook to the Queen's taste. He could even bone, stuff, and roast a chicken or turkey so we were able almost to forget that we had had chicken or turkey every day for months on end. It was the only fresh meat obtainable, aside from occasional venison, and dull custom reduced the flavor to a nausea that must be borne, rather than a delicacy for high occasions.

Unfortunately for us, one fine day Alphonso made a ten-strike in a lottery. He took in his thirteen thousand dollars, resigned as cook, and, very shrewdly realizing that there is only one way to win in gambling, and keep on winning, set up an establishment of his own in Progresso wherein he sat behind the wheel and sold the tickets himself. The next time Earl and I arrived in

Progresso he met us with a huge light-blue limousine driven by a uniformed chauffeur, and solemnly took us for a long formal drive round and round Progresso's two miles of paved streets. His manner was perfect, for in the face of what might easily have been a *nouveau riche* and blatant flourish, he conducted himself with tactful, meek discretion.

When procuring another cook to replace him, Earl inadvertently got mixed up in an economic tong war that had roots stretching as far as China itself. It seemed that there were two tongs, or factions, in Merida Chinatown, each captained by a man of real capacity. We started negotiations with one of these leaders for a full quota of cook, house boys, and laundry men, but his demands were too high, so we turned him down. Although we didn't realize the definite split in Chinese politics, it did seem as if in all Chinatown we could rake up half-a-dozen men or so that would be more reasonably satisfied. In the course of inquiry we fell into the hands of the other tong leader, who, knowing in some fashion all about the previous deal, cheerfully agreed to cut his prices and bid in lower. In the meantime it appeared that Tong No. 1 was merely haggling a bit and had full intentions of taking the plum at our price, only had neglected to tell us of it. So imagine our horror when, the day before we were leaving, we made an appointment at the hotel to look our men over and give them their railroad passes, and found both cohorts drawn up in the hall outside our door, looking daggers at each other, and doubtless feeling the keen edges of real knives thrust in their clothes.

Neither would permit the other to take the job, and after an hour's weary discussion it looked as if we were out of luck. Then a messenger dashed up, conferred with both leaders a bit, and finally they tramped up abreast and said they would compromise—split the positions to be filled among their followers, divide the salary of cook, and both come themselves! Evidently Chinese secret service had been functioning, and some "man higher up," a Merida Dr. Fu Manchu, had passed the final word. We agreed with alacrity, only wondering that the two great men would stoop to such lowly service. They proved to be excellent cooks, among their other accomplishments, and evidently considered that, for a wise man, no experience is so lowly as to be valueless.

Tarsisio was our gardener (Fig. 11). At least he was on the pay roll in that capacity, although he frequently served as sleight-of-hand performer, barber, tinsmith, and watch mender. He was a Korean—a shrewd, clever chap who was equal to any emergency, and was incidentally a top-hole gardener. He was excessively proud of his handiwork and, together with his very young son and assistant (Fig. 11), labored early and late over our vegetables and fruit. Cabbages had to be at least a yard wide to fulfill his vision of the ideal, and crops rotated with clock-like regularity so that there was always something fresh for dinner. Perhaps his crowning achievement was a wonderful seedless watermelon, produced direct from the ordinary seed. It is done by a trick so simple and yet so ingenious that I don't feel I should give away his secret.

I remember on one occasion how he startled me with a turn of Spanish I hadn't before encountered. His great trouble was a mule which lived in the neighborhood and took great satisfaction of nights among the vegetables in Tarsisio's garden. No amount of bars or stone wall served as an obstacle to the persistent animal, and one morning when he was again found in the ruined carrot bed after the place had been locked as securely as a penitentiary, Tarsisio came to tell the exasperating tale. He said, "*Esa mula tiene más ideas que un Christiano.*" ("That mule has more ideas than a Christian.") I was extremely startled till someone explained that *Christiano* meant *living person* and then I couldn't help but be moved at the apt, curt manner with which the idiom hit off an idea possessed of infinite possibility.

No tale of Chichen is complete without an account of Gustav (Fig. 3). A Norwegian sailor who had traveled the high seas since he was ten, when he came to us he brought clever hands, an ingenious brain, reckless courage, and a lovable personality which mark him as one

Fig. 21

I assist at building my house. The bony framework of the roof was constructed without a single nail, and over this the too hospitable palm thatch was laid. Note lemon tree growing inside the living room.

Fig. 22

House completed. From earliest times Maya houses have been constructed in this same fashion.

Fig. 23

THE EIGHTEENTH-CENTURY SPANISH RANCH HOUSE WHICH SERVED AS EXPEDITION HEADQUARTERS

The two little stone men at the head of the steps came from the "digs," and were affectionately if not brilliantly

of our most valued friends, and as one whose future is bound to be as interesting as his past.

The story of his coming is tangled in diplomatic complications of which discretion forbids the repetition. Sufficient may it be to say that from a not-too-distant point he heard that there were white men in Chichen Itza who were moving mountains of stone for some mysterious reason, and Gustav, with his incorrigible nose for the unusual, straightway made it his business to look us up. He asked for a job, and when he admitted that he was an experienced carpenter, Earl practically draped himself about the sturdy Nordic shoulders, for a carpenter he sorely needed. Nor were his abilities limited to that one profession alone. Whenever anything was needed Gustav could make it—with wood work, iron work, and head work he flowed into any emergency with the plasticity of liquid and the strength of steel. We got a letter recently from Dr. Morley, who is again in Yucatan, and we weren't surprised to read: "Gustav has just arrived, so everything is running smoothly again."

Year by year the place grew; water pump, electric light and refrigerator plant, bath houses, laboratories, storerooms, offices, and dwelling houses were added until it assumed the proportions of a small city. We hear that this year a little hospital for the natives has been built to which they flock from incredible distances. The latter news reminded Earl of the informal dental clinic that he used to hold regularly on pay days. It all began with old Alphonso bringing a vigorous toothache with him on one of the formal evening calls he used to pay us. Earl investigated, and found the trouble lay in the single upstanding snag which adorned one side of the lower jaw. A child could have handled the matter with a piece of string and quickly slammed door, but the timorous, gentle old Chinaman would never have dared such a drastic step. Earl reached for his pliers. "Shut your eyes, Alphonso," and the next instant the tooth, together with the ache, was dangled in front of a startled face. Alphonso was overjoyed—he fairly burbled—and in the course of the next few days so thoroughly did he spread news of Earl's prowess that on pay day, after the silver was dispensed, half-a-dozen men lined up before him on the corridor with open jaws and fingers stretching at mouth corners to indicate spots of pain. He smilingly refused, but such a tale of woe ensued that his heart was wrung. It seemed that there were no dentists in the small towns of Yucatan except for a few traveling quacks who did a poor job at everything but collecting huge bills, and so the agony of a toothache was borne by the natives as an ill for which there was no remedy.

Earl was no dentist, but he was a skillful mechanic, and he had the undivided confidence of his patients. There was a pair of forceps in the medical outfit and plenty of disinfectants, so he set doggedly to work. He had only one technique for trouble of any kind—the tooth had to come out root and branch—and by main force and craft, come out it did. His patients never budged or whimpered, and evidently the work was satisfactory, for soon they were back with their friends and families. The next year better surgical appliances and local anesthetics were brought, while Earl's reputation grew to be something, I suspect, a little short of a witch doctor's.

One season a grasshopper plague descended on the land. They came in clouds which fairly obscured the light of the sun, and day after day fresh hordes would ravage what those preceding them might have left in the young cornfields. This was nothing less than tragedy for the Indians, for on their corn depended their very lives. The food of the Maya is almost exclusively made up of flat cakes of ground corn which they pat into shape on a little stool and bake in hot ashes. Supplemented by black beans, and what wild meat they can kill, it makes up the whole of their diet. A failure of crops over any wide area, therefore, means grim starvation.

This time almost the whole of Yucatan was afflicted with the grasshoppers, and the economic situation was acute. It was particularly ironical in the case of our workmen, for they would come to us with tears in their eyes to tell that their families were starving while their pockets were weighted with useless silver.

I don't think I ever realized so acutely what living in the midst of civilized transportation means. For that is the only thing that makes money of any value at all. Silver and gold themselves are as worthless as old tin cans. They can be neither eaten nor worn as clothing. But they are symbols of possession and serve excellently as mediums of trade for the things we really do want. I saw then that swift transportation is a necessity that must go hand in hand with any extensive use of money, for our bush natives were cut off by their primitive ignorance and isolated lives from taking advantage of cornfields in other lands that hadn't felt the grasshopper blight.

We took hold immediately, cabling to New Orleans for an immediate shipment of the grain, and thereafter for the remainder of the season paid our men with that sorely needed food. It was my duty to keep the accounts of these transactions, to calculate how much each man had due in wages, to translate this into *almudes* of corn, and to check the amount as it was poured into his sack (Fig. 12). The proportion of wages devoted to the staff of life was appalling. Some weeks it all went into corn and a man would stagger off on his three-mile walk for home carrying the family rations for two weeks in one load. Other times one would say to me, "I must buy sandals, Señora. Give me corn and seventy-five cents."

The sandal purchases of the community dimished rapidly, however, after one of the men saw Earl half-soling a pair of his work shoes with automobile tire. From that time there was a steady waiting line, watching like vultures for the moment one of our cars would cast a blown-out shoe. And we were apt to find surprising traces of very civilized non-skid tracks in all sorts of unlikely places.

I have mentioned a great hailstorm which occurred on April 14, 1925. It was a cataclysm, without parallel in the annals of Yucatan, and for us the day became a fixed point in time which we used for dating, much as a biblical student regards the Flood.

On the afternoon of this day, I had been doing some painting under the shade of my thatched porch. The heat had been more than I could bear out on the works, although ordinarily my sun helmet protected me sufficiently. Only the week before, out of idle curiosity, I had taken a thermometer with me and hung it to the top of my drawing board, which my hat brim did not shade. The mercury mounted so rapidly that I was fascinated—120°—125°—129°—it was approaching the top, and I, who had no experience in the way of mercury, deliberately let it commit suicide before my eyes, for as it topped 130° the limit of the glass tube was reached and the whole thing burst wide open.

On the famous April 14th, though, the heavy hot air hung like a solid thing that one's lungs refused to pump. The sun appeared to be drawing nearer to the earth, so that we could fairly see the white burning of its molten heart. Then clouds swiftly gathered; so black and thick they were that the light of day went out with the swiftness of a dying lamp, and the smudgy world seemed as if viewed through dull green glass. For minutes the lifeless stillness of the air paralyzed the earth to dead quietude that presaged the coming of calamity. Then, with a burst, the skies opened and rain poured down. I fled for the house, slamming doors and heavy shuttered windows, hardly slipping the final latch when with the *rat-a-tat* of a machine gun bits of ice carried on a rising gale hammered against the screen. Above the continuous roll of thunder I could hear the staccato drumming of the hail growing louder and heavier, till under the impact of a particularly heavy gust of wind a bit of thatch at the roof's crest blew off, and stones larger than hens' eggs shot through the opening into the room below with the speed of projectiles.

I retreated precipitately, only to find that streams of water were pouring in under the doors of the front part of the house, so I scrambled to pick up those things which might be damaged, and tried to check the flood. First from one direction, then another, the volleys of ice and water would attack my leaky stronghold, and I remember thinking with gratification that, even though

I was swamped, I couldn't very well sink. Soon I gave up the futile job of trying to keep things dry, and waded from window to window ankle deep in hail and ice water, following the shifting lee of the storm to watch its course.

The sight was as terrible and as beautiful a one as I have ever witnessed. I wouldn't be able to see twenty-five feet away, then with a shriek the gale would shift to another quarter, and for a moment I would glimpse bare-stripped trees bending almost double before the fury.

There came a lull, then the storm rounded back on its tracks and the whole thing was repeated. Finally the curtain of ice began to lift, a few last stones dropped from some greater height, the wind ceased, and the surrounding landscape again became visible, but battered, disheveled, and strangely altered. The destruction was tremendous. Dead animals lay throughout the bush, which itself was stripped as stark and bare as are our parks in winter. For the first time, probably, since the old Mayas had turned their country into "one continuous garden," that dense wall of impenetrable green which had veiled the country was beaten down so that one could see the surface of the earth. We were startled to find old mounds that we had never dreamed of not ten feet from constantly traveled paths. For those first few days the staff ranged the environs of the city from end to end, taking advantage of the one beneficent result of the great hail. Then the vital life-force of tropic growth inexorably covered the trees once more with green and threw out tangled nets of vines again to shroud the nakedness of a land which had long forgotten what it was to be clean and bare.

CHAPTER XII

I Excavate a Temple Myself

Soon after the finding of the Sacrificial Altar in the Temple of the Warriors, the workers most unexpectedly came on a trace of a fresco painting which had one time adorned the temple walls.

In the corner where they made their discovery the walls were standing to their full original height, but this condition was an unusual one, for the collapse of the roof in most cases dragged the walls with it, and the débris from both fell together in a tangled mass of cut stone, rubble, and mortar.

The first hopes of finding paintings in a good state of preservation were shattered when digging revealed that the action of seeping water and roots had peeled almost all of the plastered and painted surface away from the high standing walls. However, from those which had fallen we were surprised to derive much better results. Although each stone had been separated from its fellows in the crash, nevertheless, at the moment of its fall, its colored surface had been in perfect condition and had so remained. Hundreds of these isolated stones, measuring somewhat more than a square foot in area, began to appear, and with them they brought a problem of the greatest delicacy and importance. This problem was turned over to me, and when I began to study it I found myself quite buried under a job from which it took me four long years to extricate myself.

It was three months, however, before the first traces of the paintings appeared—an interval of time which was devoted to work on the serpent columns, the altar, and the pyramid slopes. During that period my leisure began to weigh heavily on my hands.

I had completed my superficial sightseeing of the tem-

ples already known, and the strangeness of adapting myself to the new way of life had worn off. So, between
intervals of watching the workmen around the Warriors'
Temple, I amused myself by prowling a bit through the
bush in the cool morning hours "to see what I could
see." In the course of time these investigations led me to
a circuit of the great *cenote*, or sunken lake, which had
served the ancient city as a common reservoir for drinking water.

Somewhat back from the north bank I came on a
little mound, which, although it was completely covered
by trees and undergrowth, gave unmistakable signs of
being the remains of a man-made structure. Cut stone
lay about its foot and in the precise center of the crest
was a large stone rectangle which caught my attention
straight off, for the slanting rays of the sun brought out
on its battered top lines and curves traced with an ordered precision that no amount of tree-root action could
have produced. This was a find worth making, for it
was exactly the type of stone with which the Maya had
bridged the tops of their thick doorways when beams of
wood were not utilized for that purpose. The flat carven
side, when in its original position, would have faced
downward, and if I was right in my deductions, the edge
which had once faced outward toward the temple's
front should bear further decoration which by all prece-
dent ought to be a date. I knew how Dr. Morley felt
about dates! They were the very breath of his life, and

incidentally, they were so rare at Chichen Itza as to be almost invaluable. With fingers trembling with excitement I explored the edges buried in the leaf mold, and sure enough, I could feel the slight grooves and ridges that meant I had guessed right. I tugged at the great block in attempts to turn it, but it wouldn't budge under my frantic but futile strength. So, giving it up for the moment, I broke out of the undergrowth and went tearing down the road toward the hacienda to get a man and a crowbar.

Nobody was home but some of the native servants, and in those first few weeks my Spanish vocabulary hadn't run to such technicalities as the word for crowbar. That was an impasse I hadn't bargained for, and in my excitement I behaved as do all Americans trying to make themselves understood in a foreign language—repeated the same word over and over, louder and louder:

"Bar, *Bar*, BAR!!!"

Luck and etymology were with me, for after some puzzled minutes the gardener said, "*Oh, barra!*" and straightway fetched a hefty steel crowbar from some cache known only to himself.

Back we went to my precious stone and soon had it turned up to the light. I was sick with disappointment, for the date had been almost completely wiped out by the root action and rain of centuries, and not one sign remained legible enough to read.

After the roof fell, the great stone had evidently remained in place across the two stone jambs of the door, until a tree growing from the débris directly underneath had raised it and spilled it over wrong side up, with the two carved faces exposed to the ravages of the elements.

It was hard luck, but when I told the story of its finding that day at lunch I was gratified at the excitement I aroused. Dr. Morley came out to look, and although the poor remains of carving were beyond even his phenomenal skill of interpretation, I could tell from the way he went poking around my mound that he was much interested. The position of the building near the brink of the great pool seemed important, he said, and when between us we discovered the top of a ruined stair reaching from the plaza in front down the side of the cenote, the ceremonial relationship of one to the other appeared to be certain. Inspiration descended.

"Look here," I cried, "let me excavate this building and see what it is, and if there isn't some more carving." We sat down on the disappointing stone, and started figuring on the back of an envelope.

"It oughtn't to take long. Say two weeks for excavation by eight men at so much a day, then two weeks for repair by two masons and their helpers at such a rate of pay—the whole thing oughtn't to cost more than $250." I announced that I'd throw in the wages of a competent director free, and that the whole thing seemed such a bargain we couldn't afford not to do it. We had a superabundance of workmen at the time, and as Chichen had no small temple which had been completely excavated, the project seemed reasonable. Conferences and permissions ensued, the district was cleared of trees, and the upshot was that on the next Monday morning I was experiencing the thrill of bossing my own gang of workers on my very own mound.

The structure, whatever it had been, was fronting a plaster-paved plaza, and the first few shovels of dirt revealed two low steps which led from the bush level to the plaza floor. Half my men I put to work clearing these steps, while the rest followed the outside edges of the mound at the corner nearest the cenote. They found that the raised plaza continued around on this side, stretching to the brink of the pool and to the steps leading down the slope. Working on this level, they cut into the edges of the débris until they reached standing walls. In some cases these still remained to a height of five feet.

Seventeen feet from the front corner the south wall turned abruptly at right angles to the north, and after ten feet it veered again to the old direction. This time, though, the plaza did not continue, and the walls were built from a two-foot-high foundation platform with sloping sides. For fifteen feet they proceeded, then the back of the building was reached, and the process of clearing the rest of the outside was but a routine duplication of what had gone before. It was clear now that the structure had been built in the form of a very broad and squat capital T (Fig. 24).

As in all ruined Maya structures which had been equipped with stone roofs, the débris from the fallen roof almost exactly equalled the cubic content of the rooms. Therefore, the walls were filled to their crests with this mass, and where the walls gave way under the strain, it overflowed somewhat to the outside. Then an accumulation of dirt and leaf mold covered the whole, giving it the appearance of a gigantic graveled ant hill.

When the men working on the front of the building finished with plaza and steps, they pushed forward toward the building's interior. The first room proved to be a long columned hall measuring 14 x 53 feet. It made up the horizontal cross bar of the T. Two nine-foot wall stubs projected from either side of the front, but the greater part of its length was left open where wooden door lintels had been supported on four round stone columns. A second row of columns, six in number, extended along the middle of the room, and then the back wall was reached. This was pierced at its center by a narrower door fifteen feet wide, and across the width of it was a two-stone step which led to the higher floor plane of a second chamber, lying in the stem of the T. The two columns which once supported the wooden lintels for this door were square, and bore upon their faces elaborately carved human figures of the conventional sort found by hundreds throughout Chichen. This second room was much smaller than the first, and unfortunately was as bare as Mother Hubbard's cupboard.

I was beginning to despair, for the place was as characterless and uninteresting as a railroad section house, and certainly promised to be worth not a whit more than the few dollars we were putting into the venture. The weather was unmentionably hot, and I had to forego my usual leisurely siesta, for my well-meaning but untrained crew seemed to be possessed with a perfect genius for doing the wrong thing if left to their own devices for five minutes at a stretch.

The little building, which was rapidly taking on its proper shape because of the constant removal of débris, was situated in the center of a patch of deep forest so thick that cool breezes from outside never stirred the air wherein we worked. My brains fairly seethed in my head, and I found the only way I could get my thinking apparatus to function at all in the stifling afternoon hours was to plunge my head every few minutes in the tub of water the masons were using for their repair work, and then to wear a thin straw hat to permit rapid evaporation.

My diggers cleared the second room with the masons fast on their heels working at the preservation of shaky walls and columns. Some of the latter stood firmly in place; others had toppled forward, measuring their full length upon the floor; and some of those in front unfortunately had been robbed of their top drums, for we never could find them.

At last the second room was clean; the ultimate bit of the mound alone remained cluttered with its high-filled débris. A tiny low door gave through the wall—the door that had been bridged by the lintel of stone which had first attracted my attention. In my spare moments I had given much study to the carved face of this block. By utilizing the slanting rays of sunrise or sunset, supplemented by the more localized light obtainable from an electric torch, I endeavored to separate the pits and crevices due to work of the elements from those that were man-made. The design was tantalizingly faint, but just sufficiently traceable to lead the eye from point to point over certain paths that a knowledge of Maya sculpture made familiar. A few straight lines appeared to have blocked off the surface into small, irregularly sized rectangles. In one of the lower corners the undulating curves of a serpent's body could be detected, while in an upper segment, two human figures were facing each other across a fire burning upon an altar. No more than this could I read, but it was sufficient to strengthen my suspicion that this building was of sacred character, and not merely a rather cumbersome dwelling place.

The third and last room removed all possible doubts, for a huge altar occupied the central position, taking up almost half the available floor space. This was the

Sacred Sanctuary of Sacrifice and in the case of this temple the builders had expended upon it a lavish degree of care almost unprecedented in Maya annals. We were accustomed to walls and arches adorned with paintings, but here the vault above the altar had been deeply carved in the form of a pictured panel.

Nothing of the sort had ever been found in Chichen Itza, and I was so unprepared for the phenomenon that I gave little note to the first detached stone or two that emerged from the digging, thinking they were but another example of the hit-and-miss adaptation of stray sculptured stones from some dismantled structure so common in the city. Since the wall surfaces were smoothed over with plaster, such sporadic carvings were no bother to the mural painter who worked later.

However, a third stone markedly similar to the first in style arrested my attention. I halted the digging. "Wait, Donicio," I called to the busy little chap who was grubbing away industriously amid the cloud of dust hanging over the altar. "Where did that last stone come from?" He pointed out a depression in the black mold immediately above the temple's back wall and so near the top of the mound that a corner of it must have been visible all the time we were tramping back and forth.

"And now, where did the other two lie? I must know exactly." And he, obliging the vagaries of the white señora, who put her time to such peculiar purposes, showed me two spots, each one immediately flanking the position of the last-noted stone.

This looked promising. I twisted the stones about and found that their queer patterns joined accurately to one another. "Fine work, Donicio. Now find me some more." And for the rest of the day I hung over his shoulder, seizing on each new stone as it appeared, penciling a number on its corner, making a chart in my note-book of the position where each was found, and laying them face up in what order I could on the floor of the temple's great columned hall.

Some fitted together nicely; others seemed to bear no relation to the whole except for a similarity of style. But bit by bit the general scheme of design became evident. The center of the panel was occupied by two noble warriors standing facing each other. They were elaborately clothed, and about the body of each was coiled a huge plumed serpent. The remainder of the space was filled with the delicate tracery of vines and flowering plants, among which were fluttering tiny insects and birds. The whole thing was enclosed by a wide flat stone frame (Fig. 25).

We couldn't find all of it although the sanctuary was searched and cleaned until not a pebble the size of a walnut remained on the floor. Just enough was available to make my arrangement and schematic deductions as to its original size seem probable, but a few keystones were sorely needed to tie together some detached sections of the design. I calculated that thirty stones had originally gone into the panel. Of this number we had only twelve. I was very disconsolate because I feared that the vandals who, in some bygone age, had robbed me of my column drums had been illy inspired to lug off the major portion of my lovely panel.

Then I looked up to see faithful little Donicio rounding the corner of the temple, puffing under the burden of a stone which he deposited at my feet with all of the pride a pet cat shows in a particularly choice specimen of mouse. It was a stone of my panel, but where in the world had Donicio obtained it? "Just back of the temple where the trees are thickest," he answered to my unspoken question.

I gave hasty orders to my crew: "Come, all of you, at once, and bring your machetes." They had the undergrowth cleared in short order, and two more stones were found, the last one a good ten yards from the temple. Why they were so far from their source I never have figured out, but it immensely widened the field of probabilities.

I called the men together. "Search the bush for stones of this kind and for every one found I will give a peso in addition to your wages."

Even the masons joined in the search, and for a couple of days discipline and set hours of work were ignored in the ensuing frantic hunt. The bush was combed far and wide, and every now and then a shout would go up, "I have found another."

The boys dug over the ground much as one would a potato field, but toward night of the second day they began to filter back to their old jobs, ruefully regarding the remaining gaps in my panel, but shaking their heads over the chance of filling them. Then down the path came old Jorge Pot, his face wreathed in smiles, bearing on his head a perfectly enormous stone. It very definitely did *not* belong to my panel, and I thought I recognized it. "Where did you get this stone?" I inquired as sternly as possible. And the guileless old man answered, "From the temple the Engineer, your husband, is building. I told him you wanted it, and he agreed that I might take it, but that I must bring it back to-day. There are many carved stones there. May I have a peso for every one?" I strangled an almost overwhelming desire to laugh, for he was so in earnest, and bethinking me of his mile-long trudge between the two temples while carrying that fearful weight, I agreed to one peso for his effort, and sent him back to the puzzled Engineer, my husband, who thought I must have gone quite crazy.

That incident showed me that the possibilities for further finds were evidently exhausted, so I called back the rest of the men, and took stock of what I had. Fully two thirds of the panel were now at hand and among the recently added stones were precisely those that I required to tie together my loose sections. I regretted the loss of the rest, of course, but considering everything, thought myself very fortunate to have come out so well.

Thanks to the notes I had taken of the positions of the original twelve blocks, I had not only convincing proof of their position in the arched roof of the sanctuary directly above the altar, but also of the manner of their fall. The topmost elements had fallen first and farthest, that is, nearest the doorway, and were the most deeply buried. The successive tiers, in astonishingly regular order, had rested higher and nearer toward the base of the arch, until the lowest rows were reached, which had remained exposed upon the surface of the mound. It was these elements which were found outside and at a distance.

Finally, one day about noon, the work was completed and I dismissed my men. That afternoon, however, I spent alone at the temple, taking measurements and making some final notes. I was standing on top of the altar. In preparing to jump down from it, I seized a forgotten shovel from the top of a wall and dropped its blade with a metallic clang to the floor. Almost in the midst of my leap I paused and drew back, for the clang hadn't sounded just right. It was deep and resonant. I tapped again, this time certain that a note so vibrantly throbbing was unusual, and then as a certain possibility began to dawn on me, I excitedly sounded the floor all over the sanctuary and in the outer rooms. The curious hollow tone was to be found only immediately in front of the altar, and then I knew I had chanced upon a vault hidden beneath the plastered floor. That was not the kind of discovery I could easily keep to myself, so I fled along the path to the Temple of the Warriors as fast as my legs would carry me.

The five-o'clock bell sounded as I was in full career, and I met streams of workmen on their way home. I redoubled a pace that I had thought was my limit, took the steep stairs to the temple in my stride, and fairly tumbled into a pit where Earl and Dr. Merriam were dusting off a beautiful stone figure that had just been found. I was too breathless to speak a word, but doubtless my cheerful appearance reassured them, for their first look of alarm changed to intense curiosity. Finally I was able to gasp out: "My temple . . . hollow floor . . . in front of the altar."

The telegraphic style of communication evidently served, for Earl caught up a trowel, and they started to their feet and straightway made off for my temple.

Once arrived, Earl seized the shovel, sounded where I told him, then a few times on either side, and with a look of intense satisfaction passed the modern divining rod to Dr. Merriam. He tapped for himself, and as I watched his face I could read his reaction, for there is an unmistakable "feel" as well as sound in the vibration of metal when it voices the echo of a concealed hollow. Without words I knew they were convinced.

The plastered floor was removed, and two covering stone slabs were found beneath. When these were pried up, our eager eyes peered into a roughly lined small stone vault about two feet deep. Filtered dust obscured what might be laid there, and as Earl gently fingered it through he drew up one tiny bone, then another, and yet a third. In the failing light he carefully scanned them— then pronounced his dictum: "Human." "But . . .?" I said. "Yes," he answered slowly. "They are the bones of a baby."

Wordless, the three of us crouched there as the dusk closed in, each of us thinking his own thoughts about a race of men who could construct and adorn a temple with consummate artistry, and yet would sacrifice a baby to that temple's gods.

Fig. 24

*The small Temple of the Xtoloc Cenote, where I earned my spurs as
an excavator.*

Fig. 25

*I proudly exhibit the beautiful and fragmentary sculptured panel from
my temple to Dr. Morley.*

Fig. 26

JEAN AND I COPYING PAINTINGS IN THE TEMPLE OF THE WARRIORS

Meanwhile excavation goes on about our ears.

CHAPTER XIII

I Become a Painter

My LITTLE temple was done in record time, so after the report had been written, I moved back to the Warriors' Temple to find Earl distracted over a new complication. The painted stones which had been set as an inlay over the entire interior of the building were beginning to crop up wherever a pick and shovel penetrated. Some of them bore recognizable bits of design which were complete in themselves, and these were regarded as so much treasure trove.

Unfortunately, though, due to the large scale on which the painters had worked, the majority of the blocks, measuring from one to two feet square, carried only fragments of line and color, which were completely indecipherable. Moreover, not all of them were in perfect shape, for the painted plaster had been ripped from some of them as they broke away from their anchorage, and the impact of the fall had contributed further to their destruction. It was particularly unfortunate that the edges had suffered the most, and at the time, we thought that this would make it impossible ever to fit them back together.

It was clear that little could be done on the spot. Long and careful study would have to be devoted to them, so the question of their protection became paramount. The temple was divided into arbitrary numbered areas, each bounded by four columns, or by columns and lateral walls. The advantage of this scheme is evident on consideration of the fact that when the walls collapsed inward, the veneer of stones comprising the painted surfaces fell immediately below the point where they were originally placed. Therefore such a system delimited conclusively the relation of each stone to the wall above.

This proved to be of immense assistance later. For this reason each stone bore two numbers—the number of its area, and its own number within that area. We set them to dry, cleaned their painted surfaces as well as we could, and coated them with Ambroid—a kind of soluble glue-varnish.

The first ones were carried to a little old Spanish church which had long been abandoned, and which we had reroofed in order that it might serve as a laboratory. But as the numbers kept increasing, the church floor became full, and they were stored in the hacienda. Still the truckloads poured in, for under no circumstances could the stones be left in the unprotected temple, where one heavy fall of rain would entirely demolish the pattern. They filled the corridors and the offices and in the dining hall they became a menace to progress, occasioning a full-fledged traffic jam at every meal time. And more than this, they proved a definite hindrance to everybody's work, for at any time of day you could find some member of the staff who should have been about his business crouched in rapt contemplation of one of the stones, and after long prayerful consideration, joyously broadcasting to anyone near, "Look here, there's a snake's head on this stone!"

As every evening brought its new increment, we began to feel like the unfortunate chap who contracted to take care of two guinea pigs, and at the end of the season found himself fairly buried under ever-increasing swarms. Fortunately our stones didn't have to be fed, but it became imperative that they be housed under their own roof, so that they might leave us ours in peace and erstwhile spaciousness.

The old swimming pool that a one-time wealthy owner had once installed proved just the thing. It hadn't been used for years, and it was a simple matter to raise the height of the walls somewhat, leaving windows, to break through a door, and to put a water-tight cement roof over the whole. Then shelves were set up around the four walls, and further tiers of shelves were erected down the center, leaving an empty square of floor where the stones might be laid and studied in groups.

Each area was set up on shelves of its own, and then for the first time it began to be evident that some of the areas were most fully represented, while of others, only a few stones remained. When we checked this peculiar circumstance, we found it easy to account for, because, since the central part of the mound was piled highest with débris, the paintings under its crest would naturally have been more deeply buried, hence, more adequately preserved, while the natural course of decay which sheered away and tumbled the outer walls down the sides of the pyramid left such painted stones as remained without adequate covering. Therefore the areas representing the partition wall across the center of the temple were present in great numbers, while the rest were relatively few

Long before this point was reached, I had adopted the stones as my own. All the others were fully occupied with their various jobs, while I alone, with the exception of a little casual overseeing of the housekeeping, had nothing much to take up my time. Dr. Morley had said that the following season a painter would be added to the staff to handle the stones, but in the meantime I could fiddle with them if I liked. I did like. They fascinated me, and I bewailed an education which had dropped Art from the curriculum as soon as it ceased to be compulsory. I was rarely fortunate, however, for I had barely started on my new career when Chichen Itza was visited by a very great painter indeed, who was as generous of his time as he was skillful. Mr. Joseph Lindon Smith had spent many years in Egypt and Java copying the paintings and carvings in the old temples and tombs of those countries, and when he heard of similar things being found in little-known Central America, he packed up his brushes and casually dropped in on us one day about lunch time. "Pops" Smith is a darling who is beloved from one end of this earth to the other. He carries his passport in his delicious crooked smile, and when I found he was a painter, an archeological painter at that, I fastened myself to him with the pertinacity of a leech.

Pops took my blundering copying in hand immediately, and put me on the right track. From him I learned the all-important word "values" the first minute he looked at my work. I can remember him chuckling over a sheet, then reaching for a clean bit of paper. "Now look here, Ann, this isn't a Sunday supplement, you know. You mustn't just cover all the blue places with blue paint, and then all the red spots with red paint. They must bear some relation to one another. Values, my dear, values. And then it's all too clean—why, your paint box is *disgracefully* clean."

He fell to work on a little corner of the paper with a smudge of red and a smudge of blue, mixing slap dash all colors of the rainbow right on the paper itself, keeping up a rapid-fire comment on how this sort of painting differs from the more civilized variety. Gradually the kaleidoscope resolved itself into deep soft reds and blues perfectly related to one another and exactly duplicating the faded and beautiful old pigments on the stone. I was enchanted, and from that moment I date whatever prowess that practice eventually brought me. I became a regular fanatic on exactitude, even carrying it to painstaking efforts to catch the sharp edges occasioned by breakages in the plaster. I can remember I bestowed a diploma on myself the day a friend slid a finger nail over my smooth paper thinking the indicated raised relief must be real!

Thanks to Pops, when the artist was chosen for the

staff the succeeding year I was given the job, and for years thereafter I labored over my precious stones with almost maternal pride, seeking to bring out their good points, searching out the meaning of the ones which were most brutally scarred, and fitting them into their proper places in the great pictures of which they had originally been a part.

My very lack of formal training proved to be an asset for I had no established technique or preconceived notions to throw overboard. Thus it was much easier for me to follow with absolute fidelity the curious stylization unique to the Maya than it was for those persons thoroughly grounded in conventionalism. At bottom the Maya painters were cartoonists with a peculiar quality of line that is never found in any other place. As a result of working over their material, I became a Maya painter myself, and to this day I can't draw a picture but that it has the particular bias characteristic of that ancient art.

After Pops Smith left, I returned to the stone storage bound to cover myself with glory but not quite certain how to go about it. I had noticed when the blocks had been stowed away that those from Area 31 were very numerous and were particularly easy to decipher. There were many human heads among them and some gaudy fishes that were swimming in a blue sea crossed by wavy black lines. At that time, I never dreamed that one day I was going to be able to fit the whole thing together like a giant picture-puzzle, and really see exactly what the great expanse of wall had looked like in the days of its glory. I merely thought then that there were more interesting stones in it than in any other, and that I would copy those in my new technique.

As the days went by, my stack of paintings grew higher, for with practice I began to be able to discern meaning in those patterns which had originally looked like a hodge-podge of tangled lines and colors. Human heads were easy to detect no matter how battered the stone, for the great curve of the Maya nose in relation to a black-pupiled white eye stood out like a sign post. Fishes were distinctive also, for the Maya painter had made lovely caricatures of the finny monsters. One fine day I discovered that two perfectly circular globes of green were attached to each other and in turn to a thick brown stem—a combination which surely signified *tree*. I was just getting warmed up to the chase when our season was forced to a close on account of the rains.

When I returned the next year, I brought a fresh eye to bear on the situation. Looking over my drawings, it suddenly dawned on me that I had represented there an enormous quantity of wall, and every bit of it was ascribed to Area 31. I went off hot foot for the temple with a yardstick to find out just how many square feet the wall facing Area 31 would have occupied. My calculations came to 96 square feet, or enough space to accommodate an average of 78 stones. Then I dashed back to my stones, and, taking a census, found I had 62, or nearly six sevenths of the entire wall. I *was* excited then, for with such a proportion on hand, I was sure something could be done in the way of fitting them together. I gathered from the area all of the remaining stones which had appeared too fragmentary or pointless to be worth copying, and my brush and pencil fairly flew for a week or two until I finished them all.

I had worked out the system which would ensure the greatest accuracy. I first traced the design with pencil on transparent paper, taking care to catch whatever pattern there was with the greatest fidelity, whether I could understand it or not. Then I transferred it to heavy watercolor paper by means of carbon sheets and, using the stone as a model, sat beside it and filled in my outlines with colors as nearly as possible equivalent to those on the stone. Finally, I cut my paper down to the size of the stone, so that, when I was ready to begin arranging my sixty-two stone designs, I was able to work with exact replicas instead of with the cumbersome blocks themselves, which were too heavy for me to budge. And thankful I was that I had decided on that mode of working, for before I was finished with Area 31 those sixty-two poor pieces of paper were tattered and worn to bits with the shifting and juggling about which was necessary before they fell into order.

At this point I was blessed with a volunteer helper without whose timely aid I believe I never could

have brought the deal to its successful conclusion. Jean
Charlot had been brought to Chichen Itza to copy the
multitudinous sculptured columns with which the Temple of the Warriors was adorned. He is a French painter
who had just completed some mammoth murals for the
Mexican government, and perhaps his experience with
art on such a great scale made him intrepid in the face
of my enormous Area 31. At any rate, he jumped in to
help me and for long hot days we studied and shifted
the bits of paper back and forth, wrangling over every
move as might bitterly hostile exponents of two schools
of chess. From that day to this the battle has never completely died; a quiet lull now and then may intervene,
but for the most part the peace pacts are but deceptive
breathing spells wherein we recuperate for mightier
combat. Jean is my favorite enemy, to whom it gives me
great pleasure to acknowledge my debts of gratitude.

When the two of us began to unravel the tangle of
Area 31 we found one group of blocks to which to tie our
calculations. I had long been puzzled because half of the
stones bore a blue background and half a red one, but
twelve of them were found to carry both red and blue
divided by a heavy black line which passed horizontally
across the center. Evidently the painting had represented a sea scene in its lower reaches and a land scene
above, while the division line indicated the shore. With
this central axis established, we promptly separated our
stones according to background—a proceeding which

cut our labor exactly in half. From this point a detailed discussion of the Battle of Location would prove too lengthy to be interesting. The missing stones complicated affairs, because we had no way of knowing where the gaps would occur; but eventually the task was done. We had assembled the blocks into a coherent picture, the placing of which we even agreed upon between ourselves, and I drew up in writing an imposing report justifying the location of each single stone, which has convinced everyone who has taken the pains to work through it.

I then reduced the whole thing to a manageable size by drawing the blocks to scale and tracing on each whatever painted pattern was present on the stones when found. Lastly, I put in necessary restorations, being very careful to fill in the missing parts with exact duplications of elements found in the same area, so as not to ruin its scientific value by the injection of any purely personal imaginings.

When it was colored, the little scene gave a very adequate idea of what the painting had been when the temple was in use, and incidentally reflected a bit of actual Maya life of those times as clearly as might some magic mirror which bears upon its glass an old vision permanently arrested there.

Do you remember the painter Tuche who told the snub-nosed soldier at the gate that he was going to do a picture of the little village where they got their fish if the Chief Architect would let him? Evidently the permission was granted, for the scene he painted so long ago we rescued from its scrambled grave, and in giving it fresh life almost literally justified Tuche's sage observation that "Art is eternal."

With Area 31 successfully completed, I turned my attention to the other stones to see if I couldn't, by hook or crook, arrange them so that their original pattern would fall in some order. I was very fortunate with one little group of five in presenting the central part of a scene which, when I realized its import, sent me scuttling to the hacienda to find Earl that he might rejoice with me. For the picture was one of human sacrifice— gruesome enough in truth, but vastly important from an historical point of view. There the wretched victim lay stretched before a temple door, face distorted with anguish, ankles and wrists pinned down by two priests. Above him towered the great High Priest, gorgeously decked in fantastic richness, with knife upraised— pictured at the moment before the descent which would tear into the taut breast below. Kul-kul-kan, the Plumed Serpent God in whose honor the sacrifice was taking place, dominated the whole scene. His powerful coils streamed across the whole picture, and a curve of his body served symbolically as the altar across which the victim was laid. The scene was an eloquent recital of the once-awful power of the reptile-god which overshadowed the wretched human haplessly yielding his life in propitiation of the dread power.

Another great picture I succeeded in assembling—one which was almost twice as great as that of Area 31, although one or two gaps remained in it too large for my system of cautious restoration to permit of filling. This scene was full of action for it represented a raid upon a village of thatched huts and temples of carved stone, situated upon a lake. The upper part of the scene depicted the luckless inhabitants, who were painted in stripes, vainly trying to defend their homes, both by land and water, against some black-skinned invaders. The lower section showed the vanquished villagers, completely stripped of clothing and weapons, being driven as captives along a great red paved highway. Their arms were tied with rope, and their faces were registering a despair so violent that the painter, who evidently was on the winning side, had made the poor things look most ludicrous.

One standing wall of the lot bore enough paint on its face that the general tenor of the tale it had originally told was still decipherable. The scene was almost entirely one of water with but a narrow strip of surrounding land. Upon the surface of the waves a lively scene of combat was taking place between conventionally garbed black-skinned warriors and a light-colored people with long flowing yellow hair. The latter were obviously suffering reverses at the hands of the black painted warriors who were represented as wading in the shallows or as doing battle from a fleet of canoes bearing animal heads upon the prow. One of the light-skinned men was represented as attempting to escape by swimming but at the risk of imminent peril from a very voracious shark-like fish. Another was being dragged backward over the prow into a canoe; a third was being grasped by the hair, his face fittingly distorted by acute anguish; a fourth had his arms bound behind his back.

This type of human strikes me as being quite significant, for obviously the painter was stressing an acute physical dissimilarity between his own people and those of another sort. Incidentally, it was one of these people who was being victimized in the human sacrifice described above. The long flowing yellow hair and light-colored skin, so painstakingly delineated in both scenes, were undoubtedly meant to emphasize a difference of tribe or even of race—a device stressed, since their nudity precluded the use of details of dress as a distinguishing feature. Just what it may mean can only be a matter of conjecture, but it cannot help but bring to mind the legends common to the whole New World concerning the fair skin and golden hair of some mythical race.

With the exception of a small group of so-called "White Indians" found in Panama, a condition which is due to *albinoism*, the American Indian from the Arctic North to the far tip of Tierra del Fuego is rather dark-skinned and definitely black-haired. However, there are in America many legends of people with fair skins and golden hair, which carry in their telling a hint of an invading alien race, and one's mind is irresistibly drawn to the Norsemen who cruised the Atlantic so fearlessly, more than a thousand years ago. But if the Maya painter who did this scene was actually recording a historical occurrence known to himself and his people, and therefore taking place about 1200 A.D., of battle and the defeat of an eccentric-appearing group of strangers, possibilities become even more interesting.

Some of the areas did not lend themselves to complete reassembling, although enough could be derived from their study to suggest a mental picture of those walls as they originally appeared. While again, where only a few stones remained carrying on their surface isolated fragments of design, my constantly increasing familiarity with Maya stylization and method of representation made it possible to draw some conclusions concerning their significance.

The numerous different styles of painting to be detected among the various areas gave ample proof that many painters must have had a hand in decorating the temple walls. Evidently there was no directive control or coöperation between the painters in the matter of subjects. I could find the work of fifteen men that I was sure of, and probably there were more. Judging by the results, each man must have preëmpted a certain amount of wall surface, delimiting it from that of his neighbor by hastily drawn perpendicular lines, and must then have covered the space as the inspiration of the moment directed him. As you can imagine, the final effect was a veritable kaleidoscope.

The painters first outlined the main effects of their design with a copper red paint, courageously dashing at their white wall with the unhesitating, flexible strokes of practised artists. These outlines they filled in with brilliant flat colors, and finally, as a finishing touch, outlined a second time with vivid black. Sometimes I doubted whether the retracing of the lines was done by the same hand as the first, because of marked discrepancies between the two. Either the black was put on by someone who did not feel much responsibility toward the first draftsman's work, or else the man himself overlined with a sublimely carefree attitude toward his own original drawing.

The general purport of the painted scenes was limited somewhat by tradition, but most of the scenes were drawn from direct observation. Religion and legend played their part. However, it was quite obvious that most of the painters' attention was caught by the pageantry of daily life, colored by a lifetime's association with the mysterious and impressive temple ceremonials; he was provided with ample material for his work. Life itself as it was lived in the towering temples and village huts was caught on the wing, as it were, and imprisoned on the walls with conscious fidelity to the model.

The disjointed stones as I found them were in much the condition of uncatalogued archives which deal with a subject of which little is known. When these were classified and the many tangled threads were drawn together a fabric began to take shape which was very faithful to old Maya life.

Land and water scenes, vegetation, marine life, birds, serpents, temples, houses, pottery, as well as human beings, tattooing and body painting, hair dressing, skull deformations, and an infinite variety of costume were all revealed. Work showing costume variations proved to be very interesting. When Jean, in his study of the sculptured columns which invariably carried formal human figure representations, and I, in my frescos, began to detect certain fairly constant repetitions of costume and equipment we realized that, in cross checking the two mediums of expression against each other, we could very probably factor out certain common features which would correspond to various occupations and social classes.

Jean had the advantage of possessing material made to a much larger scale than mine, hence much more detailed; but my figures were in motion—they were actually *doing* the jobs for which they were presumably correctly costumed. For many months we shuffled our papers around, endlessly cussing and discussing the problem, till we arrived at reasonable and, we think, accurate conclusions.

The first type we isolated was the *priest*. He was invariably figured as being very old or very young— the latter probably representative of the student priests. Long hair fell loosely over his shoulders from beneath a great broad-brimmed hat hung with a blue fringe and supporting a high crown from which flowed green plumes. The body was clad from neck to feet in a long sleeveless reddish robe sewn with made beads and girdled with a belt of jade mosaic plates. The shoulders were covered with a cape solidly plated with jade, and jade was employed in the ears, around the wrists, and on the sandals, and long tubular beads of it were thrust through the nose. As if this magnificence were not sufficient, a long heavily feathered "back crest," like that of a Sioux war bonnet, hung from the hat to the ground. One hand carried a feathered shield, and the other a bowl of incense. The gentlemen dedicated to the priesthood evidently took care that their actual powers should be well substantiated by outer glories. Such elaboration of dress I consider as a most conclusive evidence of the heavy solemnity and reverence accorded to their state in Maya life.

Perhaps I should state here that jade and turquoise represented to the Maya the absolute quintessence of value. Gold, pearls—all else—shrank in their eyes to the status of pretty baubles beside those two stones. When the first Spaniards reached the coast and made presents of mirrors and metal knives, their courtesy was returned by "some pieces of dull green stone," which disgusted them beyond measure. And the tale is told of Cortez, who at first was on friendly terms with Montezuma, that every day he used to receive from the powerful king gifts of great value. One day, after Cortez had bowed and scraped pleased acknowledgment of half-a-dozen great shields wrought of solid gold, Montezuma announced that on the morrow his present would exceed all those that had gone before. Cortez couldn't sleep that night—he was so eager to collect. But when next day the servant triumphantly bore in a tray on which there was "a handful of carved green stones," poor Cortez near wept in disappointment.

A second type of human being we found it easy to detect was the *sorcerer*. Occasionally he appeared garbed in odds and ends of priestly clothing, but more often he was simply girded with a short white skirt that revealed only too clearly an ugly heavy paunch and bony knees so carefully rendered by the painters and sculptors that one wonders if they weren't taking advantage of an amusing bit of realism to cheer them at their task. The sorcerer carried in one hand a basket and in the other a living writhing snake. The stooped posture, wrinkled belly, bony limbs, and disgusting burden helped us to visualize what doddering filthy fakers they must have been.

Probably the most magnificent type we encountered was that one we called *god impersonator*, from the god-masks which adorned the headdress of these figures and covered their faces. The masks were wrought in the form of the Plumed Serpent God, and the men who wore them further assumed the disguise by painting their bodies in the manner of a snake with yellow scaled belly and plumed back. They were wrapped in jaguar skins and were heavily laden with jade, as were the priests, and carried in one hand a *baton*, or staff of office. In all probability they were the nobles of the city who thus costumed themselves on days of celebration.

In dealing with a period so warlike we expected to find pictures of the army occupying a good bit of the available space, and this proved to be the case. Only like all soldiers, these possessed one uniform with which they decked themselves for dress parade, and quite another for engaging strenuously on the field. The latter uniform consisted of a simple gee-string and two handfuls of weapons, while on dress parade the men adorned themselves in gorgeous magnificence, although still retaining the weapons. These included a shield, long spears, a throwing stick, or *atlatl*, which was used for hurling the spears in place of a bow, a fending stick with which they warded off these spears when they came in reverse direction, a quilted defensive sleeve, and sometimes a net bag which resembled a slingshot.

Sometimes we were puzzled by figures which mixed

up all the established norms of costume and almost drove us to distraction, but fortunately they were too few to interfere materially with our methodical classification. I can remember the day when I fished just such a mongrel creature out of my stack of pictures and, after analyzing with stunned amazement the extraordinary features of the painting, turned and inquired sweetly of my harassed co-worker, "Jean, what would you say if I were to show you a figure with a death god's head, a warrior's quilted defensive sleeve, a jaguar's clawlike hand, a priest's long dress, and a god impersonator's sandals?" Jean threw up his hands, stared at me with glassy eyes, and then with the single-minded purposefulness of those going quite mad, put on his hat and left the building.

My work was not to be completed with the overhauling of the temple's interior walls, for in the course of excavation around the outside of the building, fallen plaster from the north face of the basal zone revealed bits of a colored pattern covered by numerous coats of superimposed plaster. This circumstance was surprising, as the presence of fresco painting had never heretofore been observed on a temple's exterior. Investigation revealed a series of great birds, scorpions, death gods, and animals dressed up in men's clothing, all painted upon the wall and then covered by 127 coats of plaster. We removed these upper layers painstakingly with dental picks, and found the arduous labor quite worth our while.

Other paintings were discovered in the Northwest Colonnade, and finally, buried in the very heart of the pyramid, an entire new lot was found by a happy accident. The telling of that story, however, belongs to another chapter.

CHAPTER XIV

The Cenote Called Sacred

Even archeology becomes monotonous sometimes. When one is too close to anything, real perspective is often lost, and one finds oneself in the state of the man who said, "I can't see any forest here, there's only trees." Months of grinding away at a single job tires one's brain, and the isolation of an archeological camp doesn't permit of the ordinary diversions or a change of scene. The day is sure to come when every book is read at least twice, when every conceivable subject has been talked to death and there seems to be no new thing on the face of the earth.

Such a day it was, one sleepy Sunday afternoon, when Gustav and Jean were making us a call. We had amused ourselves for some time by taking a picture of a great-grandfather iguana lizard who lived with all his family in a rock pile near the porch. The old buck, one of the hoariest-looking affairs I ever set my eyes on, used to take his sun baths on a flat rock guarding his door, which was hot enough to fry alive anything but a chilly-blooded reptile. We felt very friendly and neighborly toward him and took a real interest in his growing family. He was big enough to be interesting—about a yard long—but, more than this, he was an exact copy, on a small scale, of the huge dinosaurs of a by-gone age. We waited till he had slipped down his hole a minute to tell Grandma and the children something he had forgotten; then, creeping softly toward his rock, Earl rigged the big camera with a string to the shutter, while, to get an illusion of scale, Gustav set up a tiny wooden statuette of an old Maya warrior that a clever wood-carver visitor had bestowed upon us. On the vine-covered porch we waited breathlessly, the string held

Fig. 27

Copying a dragon head from the outside of the temple.

Fig. 28

Copying carved pilasters in the laboratory on the last day of the season. That day I managed to cover a roll of paper four feet wide and fourteen feet long—an all-time Marathon record for the Fine Arts.

Fig. 29

A Yucatan by-product illustrating the use of an archeologist's leisure hours. The subject is a venerable iguana neighbor—one of our best lizard families—snapped in the company of a tiny wooden Maya warrior. On alternate Wednesdays I tell people that it's a dinosaur and a cave man.

Fig. 30

This magnificent jaguar chewed up several natives, and when Isauro finally laid him low we found a lead bullet in his neck, and another in his foot which had been fired into him perhaps a generation ago.

nearly taut. Soon our iguana emerged again, lumbered into line with the lens, and stood as stiffly motionless as the wooden warrior with his poised spear, who seemed to dwindle even more in comparison with the bulk of the great spiny-backed reptile. It was a perfect pose. The camera snapped, and we trooped out to rescue our intrepid tiny warrior before any untoward fate should befall him. The portrait of the two you will find on (Fig. 29).

Later we were very glad we had done this, because the very next week the old lizard suddenly disappeared never to return, and the place of triumph was held by a callow young chap who was fat and uninteresting. We had an unhappy feeling that Grandfather had been worsted in some terrible family quarrel below ground, and straightway, after the manner of his kind, had been eaten by the brash young one, who thereupon assumed the duties of the head of the family.

When the incident was over and we had our photograph, the four of us lay flat on our backs on the cool cement, gossiping lazily of Mayaland and the deeds we had done. Things were pretty slow and we suffered from having no new worlds to conquer—at least none that could be subjugated before work began on Monday morning. Then suddenly one of us, and now I have forgotten to whom the brilliant idea occurred, cried, "Let's go swimming in the cenote."

"No good," I replied. "I spent all morning there

chasing the black duck, and I'm waterlogged." And I remember my regretful admission: "Ambrosio Tzib finally caught it and took it home for dinner." I was sad about that duck. It was coal-black and I had found it when I went down for my Sunday-morning swim. Since it hadn't seemed inclined to fly out of the deeply sunk little lake, it had provided a nice target, although a very agile one, for my swimming efforts. I can't recommend bare hands and human water speed as ideal equipment for duck catching, but the chase had been exciting.

However, our genius answered, "I don't mean the Xtoloc Cenote, I mean the Sacred Cenote."

"Ah!" We all sat bolt upright and looked with dawning respect at this new Columbus. That was an idea! With the possible exception of a few treasure hunters thirty years before, nobody had ever swum in the Sacred Cenote, and we knew a superstitious fear of the pool had probably kept the natives well away. We looked one another in the eye, and then rose as a man.

"Bathing suits," said Jean.

"*Under* your heaviest clothes," replied the practical Earl, "or we'll be scratched to bits on the rocks and trees in the descent."

In the interval it took for us to scramble into the proper garments, let me tell you those things we knew about the "Sacred Pool" that made swimming in it a project of such exciting interest.

In more ways than one, Yucatan is a peculiar country. There are no running streams, and little water of any kind. The whole country is made of limestone, which is characterized by great holes and fissures and subterranean streams. At Chichen Itza the water table lies about eighty feet below the surface of the earth. Occasionally the thin, stone, ground surface above one of the great underground caves breaks through, and if the cave is deep enough, the fragments of the stone roof are buried in the water beneath. If the cave is less than eighty feet deep, a "dry cenote" or sunken pit results, but if it is more, a pool of water, roughly circular in shape, with sheer straight walls eighty feet in height, is the consequence.

These cenotes form the only water supply of Yucatan, and wherever they are located there too invariably are to be found traces of an ancient Maya city. Chichen Itza was especially favored, for it boasts two of these wells, each more than usually large. One, called the Xtoloc Cenote, or "The Well of the Iguana," has served as the city reservoir from time immemorial. Steps of cut stone at one time led from its brink, winding down the curving side to the water level. To-day these have disappeared and a steep rough path is all that remains. However, when the water level is low, as it becomes in a very dry season, a few squared and smooth blocks can be seen below the water's edge.

As we had our own clean well and pump, and since

health dictated boiled water from that source alone for drinking, we put the old Iguana's Cenote to a very pleasant use. It was a great swimming pool, and one a hundred times more spectacular than any man-made pool that ever was constructed.

It is almost circular and measures about a hundred and fifty feet in diameter. Its depth is great and has never been measured. The straight sheer sides, full eighty feet high, enclose the little green lake like a great chimney. When one is lying on one's back in the water, a human being seems dwarfed to nothingness in comparison with the grim walls, which, although they are perpendicular, appear to lean and threaten the poor lone figure that dares to play within their bounds.

Great trees overhang the brink, ferns and creepers cover the cliffs, and lilies and priceless orchids are tucked into every crack. The shrill notes of brightly colored tropic birds which fly high over your head seem like voices from the good familiar world left far behind. For an hour or two at midday the sun flecks the water into cheerfulness, turns the green shrubs to gold, and warms the almost perpetual chill, but at other times the pool lies still in heavy twilight.

Staff swimming parties were very popular during the hot weather, but although the subject was never discussed in public, swimmers very rarely ventured down alone, and never went back, once they had. It was just one of those things that weren't done. The spirit of the place lay too heavily on one, or perhaps the memories of bright voices and tinkling water jars which once had crowded the steps brought with them too close a realization that even as those jars lay now broken upon the earth, so also were the once living voices shattered and gone forever.

The second cenote, somewhat larger in diameter than that of Xtoloc, has never been so frivolously treated. No steps lead to the water, and no rope grooves are cut into the rocky brink to mark the hoisting places of old earthen water jars. Visitors tiptoe to its edge, gaze wonderingly into the murky depths with a sort of fearful curiosity, and then draw back to talk in instinctively lowered tones. For this one is that cenote called Sacred, and it holds in its heart a mystery and a horror that have survived the lapse of centuries (Fig. 31).

Trees and clinging vines drape its clifflike sides, and in cracks among the roots sluggish lizards lie in homes they feel to be forever safe from human interference. The water is jade-green in color, and is of a texture that seems ominously thick and heavy when viewed from the brink so far above.

Long ages ago this pool of mystery held central place in a religion of terror that gripped all of Central America and Mexico in its ruthless talons. The gods of old America were foul and horrible beyond thinking. Their very shapes were deformed conceptions of loathsome reptiles, fierce-toothed animals, and vicious-beaked birds. Their minds were the diseased mentalities of slobbering idiots, maddened demons, corpse-tearing harpies, and blood-snuffling snouted beasts.

To such gods the Maya of Yucatan offered their prayers—prayers that could have been little else than a whimper for mere life. And that life, when granted, became in turn nothing but constant placation of the corroded souls of never-satisfied gods. Anything, everything, was submitted frantically to appease their sullen hatred of the race of man. Great temples were built for their glory; the smoke of a thousand fires of incense rose in their honor; captives were slashed bloodily and their beating hearts were brutally torn from still-conscious bodies as triumphant offering; but the Sacrifice of Sacrifices was the gift of lovely maidens who were thrown living to the great god of the Sacred Pool—a murder supposed to mean death in honor, but which was, nevertheless, a death of unspeakable horror.

The most beautiful young girl was chosen. She was sought from far and wide over the whole land, and she who was highborn, most fair, and most gentle, was doomed to be the bride of the god.

In the cool light of early dawn, the procession slowly descended the steps of the great central temple (Fig. 6). In its midst the luckless maiden, beautifully clad and hung with jewels, moved, half mesmerized and but little conscious of the glorious pomp with which she was surrounded. First came the High Priest—a man of royal blood, stooped under some deep sadness. His flowing hair was surmounted by a heavy crown of colored plumes. A robe of heavy red woven stuff sewn with jade reached to the ground, and in his hands he bore a beautifully fashioned bowl of smoking incense. Behind him came the lesser priests—those who were students and neophytes of the famous lore known to the priests of the land alone. These were followed by bent and aged sorcerers, vile and wrinkled, who held living snakes writhing in their hands. Then came the nobles of the realm dressed in the manner of the gods themselves—with bodies painted like serpents and faces covered by grotesque masks which towered three times repeated above their heads. And then the captains of war, martial in bearing, and proudly gripping the weapons of their trade.

Behind followed the servants of these stately masters bearing gifts for the god—an assembled wealth of gold and precious stones and artistry unequaled in the kingdom. And after these came the rabble of the city.

With drums beating a muffled Dead March the procession passed majestically down the Sacred Causeway —a road straight as an arrow which led from temple to pool. The heavy, low-voiced chant persisted as the Sacred Pool was reached, and the spectators ranged themselves around the brink. The High Priest entered the small temple there, while neophytes kindled the great blaze which rose aloft in a roaring column of flame, to proclaim far and wide that to-day the god should receive his bride.

Then one by one the great stepped forward with their gifts in hand.

"To you, O God of Rain, and to you, O God of Death, and to you, O God of Battle . . ." the litany swelled as a thousand throats carried it on . . . "I give this bowl of the yellow metal of the sun. For your honor, for your glory—and may you grant me Life." With the last shrill word the giver drew back his arm and flung the bowl of solid massive gold far into the center of the Sacred Pool. A pause while all watched its twisting descent, a smashing crash at the impact of the water, full eighty feet below, and it sank slowly—glittering for a few instants, then passing into the thick green shades and oblivion.

Another took his place with a rope of beads of jade. Apple-green and translucent they were, and finely matched, each smoothed and carved in a wondrous manner. Near a lifetime of work to make each bead—a necklace that had been in the family since the Maya race was young—it, too, was consigned to the gods.

A prince of the realm took his golden crown twined with wrought serpents from his head—a warrior rubbed a hand in a last caress over his most cherished weapon, carved from smooth black wood, adorned with plumes and set with turquoise—the priest of bloody sacrifice seized from his belt a knife of sharp black volcanic glass from Mexico, with a handle wrought of golden twisted rattlesnakes: all these sung through the chill morning air as earnests of the good will of the gods.

Excitement ran higher among the folk ringing the pool—even a baby, hanging to his mother's skirts and clutching with free hand a beloved doll with arms and legs that moved on joints of rubber, ran to the brink and cast it in, then turned weeping away.

Sudden silence as the High Priest slowly emerged from the temple, taking from his pouch what was probably the most sacred thing in all his possession. It was a small sphere of jade about an inch and a half in diameter, and it had mystic properties of singular power for these superstitious, magic-ridden people. It was called a *zaz-tun*, or "light stone," and in it the priest would read the future and the will of the gods. Holding it high in his right hand and with a ball of burned charcoal in his left, he called in a loud voice, as he cast them in:

"Hear me, O God of Life and Death—god who is Master of Light and Lord of Night. I return to you your two eyes. For twenty years I have served you faithfully. I have tried to read your wishes in your eye of light and hope, and I have sacrificed much blood to this, your other eye of darkness and despair. But now, O Master, I return them unto you, for the stone of light will speak to me no longer. Another will take my place before your altars. To-day one last gift I make to you—the fairest maiden in all the land—she who is highborn and good and gentle."

Here his voice broke, and none but the nearest heard the end: "I give to you my daughter and my only child."

He stepped back and gestured to the fragile girl's two attendants, who drew her to the brink. Almost like a sleep walker she seemed, with wide dark eyes fastened on her august father's face. At a sharp guttural ejaculation from one of those near by, she glanced into the terrible void below. Then panic seized her, she screamed in dreadful terror, and the next second was flung far out from the edge. Down and down, with cries strangling in the swift swirl of heavy air—a sickening impact, a floating white veil, and the surface of green water closed over forever while the fair young body sank slowly.

"God of Darkness, I pray that I may never see again," and a second time the broken old priest whispered: "My daughter and my only child." He pulled his flint knife, deliberately drew the sharp blade across first one eyeball then the other, and stood with the blood streaming down his face, while the Itza nation gazed stricken and aghast.

Of such scenes, a hundred times repeated, is made the history of the Sacred Well. When the Spaniards arrived in Chichen Itza, and found it almost deserted by its kings and people, the few campers who still lived around in the old buildings told them these stories and showed them the pool. But the Spaniards were skeptical, and although one of them repeated the main facts briefly, he prefaced it by a cautious "They say."

When archeologists studied the chronicle, they were even more skeptical, because such a thing had never been heard of elsewhere. It remained for Mr. Edward Thompson, who was for a time United States Consul to Yucatan and loved the country so that he decided to make it his home, to take the old rumor seriously. He bought the plantation house at Chichen Itza, a Spanish outpost built in the early 1700's. On his estate was almost the entire Maya city I have been describing, so he in his turn, in these prosaic modern times, became the reigning king at Chichen Itza. Rather a romantic fate for a Yankee of the Twentieth Century!

Don Eduardo, as he is affectionately called over the length and breadth of Yucatan, had full faith in the old legends of the well. He lived them by day, dreamed them by night, and finally, by the sheer force of persistence and his own belief, interested a museum in the United States in financing the work.

Then his troubles really began, because, granting the treasure was there, the problem of how to get at it fairly stumped him. Draining the pool was out of the question with the funds in hand. In addition, although that would have been the ideal method, there was some doubt whether the water would not seep back as fast as it was pumped out, considering that the under structure of Yucatan is so full of streams and fissured rock. He finally decided to dredge, imported the apparatus, and set it up on the brink, very near the stone platform whence the maidens were reputed to have been hurled.

Don Eduardo has told me the tale of those early days of dredging, full of heartbreaking anxiety and back-breaking work. Load after load of mud and muck would come up, and be frantically pawed through, with nary a thing in its mass but rotting leaves, decayed twigs, and fallen trees. We know now that he was but skimming back the accumulated débris that the years had dropped through the centuries since the great days of the Itza Empire. But at that time it seemed as if he had poured dollars and labor and dreams into nothing but a muddy pool.

Day after day went by—week after week—and still there was nothing to show but an ever-growing pile of filth and silt. Then one day two white balls of something appeared in the muck. Thompson pounced on them, felt them, smelled them, tore one open and touched a match to its heart. A long spiral of sweet-scented smoke curled upward, and I have heard that he shouted and danced like a child. For his finds were ancient balls of *copal* gum that the old Maya had used for incense. That may seem tiny finds to us but for him they spelled victory, the vindication of his fiercely believed dream.

After that every dredge load brought up something new. A delirium of excitement seized him—and who can blame him? Divers were brought for close work on the bottom, and the pile of archeological wealth grew in his strong room to be as high as the fruitless heap of original mud.

Five golden basins and cups, two score beaten and decorated large flat dishes of gold, twenty finger rings of the softest, purest ore, a serpent-decorated throwing stick of gold, a mask, shields, sandals of thin gold, a score of animal figures, and a hundred bells also of gold. All these were rescued from the well. Besides, there were bucketfuls of broken bits of the precious metal—truly a king's ransom.

Hundreds and hundreds of jade beads, large and small, both carved and plain; jade statuettes; scores of pendants and ear ornaments and carved jade tablets; turquoise inlay work, knives and beautiful flint spear-heads, thin and sharp as razors; large stone statues; finely worked pottery; pieces of richly woven cloth, water-preserved through the centuries; and a thousand more things that are fascinating to archeologists.

Among these treasures were really found those six objects which you will recognize: ". . . a bowl of solid massive gold . . . a rope of beads of jade. Apple-green and translucent they were, and finely matched, each smoothed and carved in a wondrous manner . . . a golden crown twined with wrought serpents . . . a warrior's cherished weapon, carved from smooth black wood, adorned with plumes and set with turquoise . . . a knife of sharp black volcanic glass from Mexico, with a handle wrought of golden twisted rattlesnakes . . . a doll with arms and legs that moved on joints of rubber . . . and a small sphere of jade which had mystic properties and was called a *zaz-tun*."

All these Don Eduardo found, and more than these lie still buried in the floor of the Sacred Pool. If a way were ever found of draining out the water, and keeping it out of this storehouse of the ages, I believe the world would stand aghast at the richness of bullion and treasure that would be revealed.

In spite of the lure of the gold, a find of more human interest was the discovery of skeletons so smooth and delicately formed as to leave no doubt that they were those of young girls. This was the last bit of evidence needed to confirm those old fantastic stories of the Sacrifice of Maidens.

Thirty years had gone by since the brief interval when the clatter of winches and splash of the dredge had disturbed the stillness of the pool. The ominous sense of dead things hung once more over the scene, and the water that appeared so inaccessible was again cluttered with fallen trees and rotting leaves. To swim across the pool's historic waters was, then, the rash objective of Jean and Gustav and Earl and myself.

The afternoon was sticky hot as only the tropics can be. The season of rains was at hand, and about noon a premonitory drenching shower had saturated the land-scape. When the black cloud flurry had cleared away, the sun beat down with summer intensity on thick wet bush unbrushed by the least breeze. Hot vapor rose stiflingly as the country boiled itself dry again. Maintaining United States vigor and ambition in the face of such a climate required a definite act of will—an effort which became increasingly difficult as the weeks wore on.

It was more than a mile to the Sacred Cenote, so to conserve effort we took the Ford dump truck—a gesture which appeared shamefacedly lazy, but was really a very wise move, for before that day was over we were to need every ounce of effort, every calorie of energy, that was in us.

First we made sure that the dumping mechanism was tightly locked, for the week before a near tragedy was barely averted when a truck load of human native freight we were taxiing to the railway had been unceremoniously dumped in full career by the wayside (Fig. 11). Nothing but badly skinned backs and arms and legs resulted, but the hacienda corridor was still serving as improvised hospital, and our apprehensions were alert.

The noisy mechanism clattered down the road to the Castillo, the chief temple of Chichen, then we turned into the Sacred Way, the causeway that runs straight as an arrow from temple to pool.

Once arrived, we took out an ax and a coil of stout rope and searched for a likely spot to make the descent. There was no convenient footpath as in the swimming cenote. The cliffs here were sheer and forbidding, so trees and vines had to serve as improvised ladders. Only one tree seemed at all feasible, and it was growing from a tiny ledge about thirty feet below the brink. Below this we could not see, as the sides of the pool were decidedly undercut from this point downward. However, we felt that if we could get that far, lucky accident might help us further. The major difficulty lay nearer at hand, for the tree trunk reached our level a good eight feet away from the edge of the bank. This problem was met by the cutting of a long pole which was laid from the bank edge to a crotch of the tree about six feet below— an extremely sloping and perilous bridge.

The vital question as to who should go first was solved by Earl's immediately gripping the slippery pole bridge with knees and hands and half hitching, half skidding to the friendly tree. Once started on that first descent, gravity straightway took care of any trepidations and hesitations. To start was to arrive, if you kept your balance and grip. From that point, getting to the ledge was nothing but a matter of climbing down an ordinary tree.

In another minute Earl called back: "There's a fine root that goes from here all the way down." From the confidence in his voice I had to deduce that the word *fine* meant *excellent* and not *thin and hairlike*. At the time I visualized a root as resembling the threadlike anchorage of some garden plant and was quite unprepared for a tree root which was a twenty-foot cable, rigid, strong, and as large as a person's two hands could comfortably encompass.

He let himself down below the base of the tree and slowly disappeared from sight, searching with anxious knees for the root which hung a good bit closer to the cliff wall than did his hand grip on the outjutting ledge. This part of the business was exceedingly difficult, as I was to discover for myself later. Then down the smooth root, like descending a fireman's pole, and his feet touched gratefully a shelf of solid ground which sloped to the edge of the water.

I started breathing again with relief, for I had little desire to see my good comrade and husband sacrificed to a Maya god. But the respite was short-lived, for he shouted back, "Ann, it's your turn next."

Now you will hear the story of the great coward who lives in my heart side by side with the spirit that loves to go places and do things. That cowardice is a great nuisance to me, for taking mean advantage of my slight muscles and easily dizzied head, it freezes the marrow of my bones and turns my blood to thinnest water at the times when I most need my physical powers. The fact that I have always come out all right so far never seems to encourage me as a fresh emergency arises. Each time anew I descend into a very Hell of Fear, and each time it makes me hate myself the more.

On this occasion the fear must have been worse than ever, for my mind, with kindly intent, has taken its own steps to protect me from the memory. When I came to think out the details of this experience I found that every scrap of my own part in it had disappeared completely. Although I remember the details of what happened before and after perfectly, and my experiences when in the well, the intervals of descent and ascent are wiped clean from the mental slate. Earl told me as well as he could what happened, but the story is rather uneventful.

It seems that Gustav slung a noose around my shoulders and under my arms, wrapping the rope around a strong green sapling on the brink. Then he paid it out slowly as I went down—a safety measure that the stricken part of me must have deeply appreciated. The first thirty feet or so went off all right, till I came to the base of the tree, then the underslung root proved inaccessible to my groping feet. If I couldn't grasp it with my knees and so pull myself in toward the rock wall, I would drop straight into the shallow water's rocky edge. My efforts to grasp it caused me to slip till tight fingers alone had a hold on the ledge, and still my feet struggled out of reach of the saving root. Earl rescued me then in the nick of time. He swarmed back up and with his hands hooked my heels around the root, and then, as much by moral support as any actual help, enabled me to bend, feet first, under the shelf and to change my hand grip from ledge to root. From then on it was clear sailing to the bottom. I stepped out of the noose and watched for the others.

Jean had been boxing champion of his regiment in the French artillery, and so had claim to a strength of arms and shoulders belied by his present profession. While for Gustav, who had furled topsails in all the Seven Seas, the descent was little more than routine.

Once the four of us were safely perched on the narrow strip of beach at the water's edge, we stripped to our bathing suits and looked around. The effect was good from an artistic standpoint. But a glance back at the only means of getting out again was far from reassuring. However, I deliberately put it out of my mind for the time and poked an exploratory toe into the water. It was gratefully cool, so we all hopped in.

A yard from shore, the bottom, for all practical purposes, became non-existent. Forty feet deep, the water was, with forty feet under that of soft oozy mud before solid stone was reached. We were all swimmers, though, so it didn't matter. In our slow swim back and forth across the pool, thoughts of the treasure beneath and the maidens' whitened skeletons dragged heavily against natural buoyancy. Then directly under the platform whence those old sacrifices had been hurled, I made a delightful discovery. A long thin root hung free from a tree at the overhanging brink clear to the water's surface. At its base it sprayed out in a little cluster of tentacles which sucked at the life-giving water and pumped it to the great tree forty feet above. When I grasped this little knot and swam as far back as I could, lifting it as high as my arm permitted, the root was pulled many yards out of plumb. Then I could lie flat and quiet on the surface of the water, and the root, in an effort to achieve its original perpendicular status, would whiz me through the water at motorboat speed. Back and forth it swung in shortening sweeps like a great pendulum, till it once more hung straight and still. As you may imagine, that root became instantly popular. I tried to work a "finder's keepers" dodge for a while, but I was out-voted. Strict communism was set up then and there in the bottom of the Sacred Well: a far-flung arm of Moscow that would have startled the followers of Lenin, had they known.

Too soon we realized that, although still early in the afternoon, twilight was beginning to settle upon our sunken little soviet. The problem of getting out had to be met and that right quickly. We scrambled back into our tree-torn clothes, and Gustav made for the famous climbing root. Going up was a slower matter than coming down. The full tide of gravity had to be fought instead of merely restrained, we were all tired from our strenuous play in the water, and, worse than all, our hands were water-soaked so that they were too smooth for an effective grip.

Gigantic puffings ensued, there was a shower of small pebbles, miniature avalanches of dirt, and broken branches and twigs dropped in quantities sufficient to build a beaver's dam. After a while all was quiet, so Earl took his turn, then Jean; and following an interval when they all caught their breaths, down came my rope. In that period of anxious waiting, while I was there alone, the gray shadows had grown deeper, and the well took on its old look of dreadful mystery. I didn't feel at all comfortable, and one knee began to jerk spasmodically.

I heard Earl's voice faintly from above: "Tie the rope well." This I did in a huge clumsy knot that would have served to hold six of me securely. But unfortunately I neglected to make the loop which passed under my arms small enough, nor was the error discovered till it was too late to correct it. Once again the blank of memory intervenes—with only a single recollection. When under the strain of transferring my grip to the outjutting ledge, I remember feeling the rope start to slip over my straight upreaching arms. I can visualize now just how serious this was, because if it had slipped a few inches farther, the loop over my shoulders would have passed over the back of my head, and with the constant pulling strain exerted by the three men above the knotted front would have ripped my hands from their hold. Instinctively I did the only possible thing under the circumstances, for with a frightened yelp which warned the three above to hang on tighter, I threw my head back, let go with both my hands, bringing my arms down sharply to stop further slipping of the rope, and clutched for dear life at the knot. This threw my whole weight upon the rope alone and I dangled, twisting dizzily clear of the cliffs. From that moment I was out of the picture as an active agent in the ascent. I hung, a dead weight, scared almost into insensibility, while inch by inch I was dragged back into the living world. I discovered later from bruises and scratches all over my body that I must have banged again and again against the rough rock cliff, and that branches must have gouged and cut painfully, but at the time I felt nothing. My whole soul was concentrated in the grip of my hands on that rope, and they tell me that when at last I was hauled over the brink I had no power myself to unclench them. The men had to bend back those fingers one by one to free them from their terrific grip, for they were, quite literally, starkly frozen in position.

Then memory comes back again, and I see myself sitting on the ground, breathing live air and rejoicing in the warmth of the sun upon my back. Never before had the forest appeared so richly golden green, never had bird notes sounded so sweet. For me it was a new world, beautiful beyond anything I had ever imagined.

The very soil seemed friendly; I remember scratching up a handful of gravel and dirt with my bruised fingers and holding it closely, the way one would some priceless treasure. For those few minutes, the scales of the commonplace fell from my eyes, and I saw the earth and loved it, in the manner that one should.

CHAPTER XV

The High Priest's Grave

ANCIENT people the world over seem to have had one constant feature in their religion. This was a belief in immortality—the life of the soul beyond the grave. And almost invariably the conception seems to have

Fig. 31

THE SACRED WELL

It seemed impossible to secure a satisfactory photograph. It is too deep and too narrow to permit the proper focus, nor could any camera catch the threatening spirit of mystery that broods over this grave of countless young maidens and blood-stained gold.

Courtesy of Carnegie Institution

Fig. 32

A GREAT CREMATION PIT FOR HUMAN BONES

*Found directly beneath one of the columns at the base of the Warriors'
staircase. The situation called for their removal with the least possible
disturbance of the heavy carved column.*

taken on a practical aspect. They believed in caring for the soul of a person who had departed this life in much the same way that they would provide for an infant. For even as a child is unable to acquire those things for itself which make life possible, so also the soul was regarded as a helpless thing, without the necessary hands by which to maintain its existence. For, to primitive men, hands were the most useful and important things in their life. Hands, indeed, are what made them men.

The ramifications of this basic idea of soul survival were many. Sometimes, it would seem the ancients believed that this period of helplessness was very short, and hence that the soul needed assistance only for that brief, difficult journey to the place of next residence. While in other districts the feeling of responsibility by the living for the dead went on indefinitely.

This sense of responsibility took a very practical form. The dead were placed in more or less elaborate graves, and they were provided with food and drink for their sustenance, and with clothes and personal ornaments. Weapons for hunting were provided sometimes, and often the tools of the person's trade were given to him for his soul's use.

Even animals which had been especially beloved were cared for in this manner. A couple of dogs buried by the Basket Makers of New Mexico were provided with deer bones for their consumption in the future world, while Earl and I ourselves found a splendid old eagle's tomb wherein he was carefully covered by a beautiful basket; provided with a quantity of the very choicest lizards and mice to sustain his spirit, and even given a string of lucky beads to wear around his neck.

From this foundation the idea appears to have been further developed, though in most cases of this kind we have to rely upon logical deduction and even sheer guesswork. For after a race of people is once lost from the face of the earth, if they have left no detailed writings about the manner of their thinking and acting, the archeologist has to piece together as best he can such facts as he can acquire. But with rather clever detective work, he sometimes succeeds astonishingly well in following his clues to reasonable conclusions.

The purely practical aspect of providing a grave with furnishings of all sorts was sometimes swallowed up in more spiritual motives for the act. Sometimes, it would seem, gifts were placed in a venerated grave by those bereft, much as tribute was offered a living king. Again, those little treasures which the dead person had once loved were given him to keep forever, from pure sentiment. Amulets and charms are often found which open up speculation into the mystical. They were undoubtedly considered to be of definite benefit to the soul in its future life, but whether they exerted their influence to placate dreaded powers or served somewhat as countersigns of entry to a distinctive or favored spirit-realm, we can only surmise.

The general idea is older than we have any means of knowing. A formally equipped burial of a Mousterian skeleton is recorded from France. Mousterian man lived many, many thousand years ago, and possessed a head of contours so heavy and misshapen and apelike that he barely resembles man at all. But evidently even in his rude brain certain dim conceptions existed of honoring or helping that indeterminate part of man that did not die, even when the body grew cold.

And so down the ages the custom has persisted, leaving under the soil of the world countless millions of prepared entombments, each one a tiny reflection of the customs and possessions of the folk among whom that man or woman lived and died. Such burials are priceless to the archeologist, who studies for yet more and more light on the past life of man. Knowledge of the future is perhaps fortunately veiled from our knowing, because we could not understand. But knowledge of the past lies in many piled layers beneath our feet. And to him that searches shall it be revealed.

Great riches are not necessary to give value to such graves. A tiny roll of tin found in Machu Picchu, Peru, which proved that the forerunners of the Incas intentionally manufactured bronze, was of more real value to the scientist than the treasure of pure gold which burdened the later ancient cities of that country.

A truthful Egyptian coin which carried portraits of

Antony and Cleopatra—showing, alas, the lady-killing Roman to have a double chin and the world-renowned queen of seductive beauty to possess a thick upturned nose with a bump on the bridge—is probably of more malicious interest to the world to-day than the pretty statues of all antiquity.

The diet of the Stone Age people of northern Europe had been worked out by clever deduction as consisting almost exclusively of hard tough meat, because so many of the skeleton joints show traces of severe rheumatism, while the jaws are invariably deformed as a result of arduous chewing.

In the Canyon of Death in Arizona we found the body of a turkey, a thousand years dead, which had a broken leg. Someone had prepared careful splints and bound them in place, and healing had already begun before the bird died. This implies a degree of experimental surgery well borne out by the skeleton of a strong-boned adult man found near by. At an early period in his life both shin bones had been broken clean across in some way not difficult to imagine in that dangerously rocky and deep canyon. Both had healed excellently, with only small bony knots to show the places of fracture. Surgical skill had made possible many years of active life to this old Basket Maker, and the cleverness in bone setting revealed an extraordinary medical knowledge for so primitive a people.

Sometimes burials of an established type are accompanied by some object that has no business at all in that bailiwick. And such things are an eloquent testimonial to the extensive travel that went on in some by-gone age.

Hundreds of such instances have been recorded. Copper bells of Aztec design found in New Mexico speak of trade with the Valley of Mexico more than a thousand desert miles to the southward, while in reverse direction the turquoise for a wonderful mosaic disk we discovered in Chichen Itza itself must have been mined in our own Southwest.

Obsidian glass traveled from the Yellowstone to Ohio, while *abalone* and *olivella* shell beads and pendants from California are strewn from the coast to Texas.

A sea shell from the Mediterranean was found in a Stone Age grave in Norway, and a bronze dagger of later date from that same country found its way clear to the shores of the Black Sea.

When Pizarro first landed in Peru he found there a greatly venerated bird which was nothing less than an ordinary European hen. The chick had arrived overland from the recent Portuguese settlements on the east coast of Brazil. The journey involved a crossing of the broadest and most difficult part of the continent—up rivers, through jungles, and over the highest range of mountains in America.

Of course, some of these transfers may have been the result of tribe-to-tribe barter, and their long journeys consumed slow years. But for all of that, it is sufficiently

proved that vast distances possessed no terrors for prehistoric peoples. A transcontinental walking tour was
evidently a matter of no great importance, even when
the traveler was burdened by the possessions he was
bent on planting in some foreign soil to the mystifi-
cation or edification of future archeologists.

Before we ever arrived at Chichen Itza, Dr. Morley
and Earl spent some happy useless hours speculating on
the burials to be found in that city. As I remember it,
they decided to leave the common people out of their
searchings altogether, and to concentrate on princes
and priests alone. Though just how they were going to
be so selective, when the same type of dirt and leaf
mold covered all alike without snobbish caste dis-
tinction, I don't believe they said.

Elaborate calculations were indulged in. Chichen
Itza was supposedly inhabited for so many years . . .
now, granting a certain span of life to each incumbent
. . . and this many contemporaneous members to the
royal family, and that many to the upper hierarchy of
the temples . . . such and such a number ought to be a
minimum at least. They were pretty conservative, but
at that, the quantity of possible tombs, replete with
treasure of greatest archeological interest, made our
mouths fairly water in anticipation.

But we should have remembered the proverbial
danger of counting one's chickens before they are

hatched. For not one of those particular chicks is hatched to this day, and no amount of thoughtful incubation or arduous labor has been able to produce even so much as a single peep. The centuries' deposits of decayed vegetable matter and earth keep safely intact those burials they have in trust.

We have searched into mounds both big and little; we have sounded the floors of temples for betraying cavities, and dug in front of altars; we have tunneled into pyramids and ransacked natural caves. Here and there, in sheer desperation, we have dug holes into the flat traceless ground, earnestly hoping that our luck might serve where logical reasoning had failed. But nary a prince or priest has rewarded our labors. One large cremation pit was found at the foot of the steps of the Temple of the Warriors, which might account in part for our failure, but this evidence of disposal by burning is unique. I would gamble on it, that the majority of graves are still somewhere in Chichen Itza, and you who read this book may some day have the fortune to find the secret of their hiding places. (Fig. 32)

The once-despised common people proved more accessible, but only slightly so. You may remember I told you of finding a few bits of a baby's skeleton buried in the little stone crypt before the altar in the temple I excavated. However, this sacrifice was evidently not repeated elsewhere, nor was that baby provided with any objects which could withstand the decay of time.

The body of an adult was found in a curious bottle-shaped pit called a *chultun*, clay lined, which may have once served as a water reservoir. This person, however, had no equipment at all, and it is barely possible he was murdered and thrown there in relatively recent times.

Another body, accompanied by three crude pots, was found in an old cave. A mass of skeletons, exhumed from their original resting place and huddled without order, were discovered lying against the foundation of the Astronomical Observatory. With such few exceptions, little trace of graves was to be found.

Only one really spectacular tomb has ever been recorded from the city, and the story of its finding is a thrilling one. Long years ago, when Thompson was working among the ruins he then owned, his attention was drawn to a hollow floor in the central portion of a small temple perched upon a forty-foot pyramid. When the stone flagging was lifted, a square cavity about three feet wide was revealed. A thick network of tangled roots masked the entrance, which, when cleared, dropped in sheer blackness an unknown depth below. A stout pole was laid across the top and a long rope fastened so as to dangle into the stone-lined shaft. An adventurous native started slowly down, but soon met further criss-cross roots which swarmed with vicious scorpions. When this dangerous obstacle had been removed, he slipped cautiously on, till, with a terrified yell, he whizzed up again with more speed than was thought possible to an amateur rope climber.

When he could talk, he narrated a tale of almost reaching what he thought was the bottom, as well as he could judge in the dim reflected light from above. But suddenly this floor heaved itself into life, a mass of writhing coils, and a huge weaving head with gaping jaws reached for his bare feet, which he managed to draw up just in the nick of time.

The proposition didn't sound good to anybody then, and the bottom of the hole achieved a marked unpopularity among the explorers. Stronger light was reflected from a mirror into the depths and field glasses revealed the monster to be an extraordinarily large snake. Fortunately, he was not a rattler with sure death lurking in his fangs, but only a species of boa constrictor which does not attack men. He was easily killed by a courageous volunteer, who in his gingerly method of descent showed only too plainly that he had no great flair for snake pits, even when the inhabitants had a reputation for harmlessness. The great slippery body was tied to the rope and hauled up —and a gruesome sight it must have been to see the whole fourteen feet of its dead length slowly dragged over the brink.

For the moment all seemed clear, so Thompson himself descended to investigate matters. The serpent's bed was a mélange of broken pottery and human bones. Slow, careful work revealed that originally there must have been two graves here, one above the other, separated by stone slabs and each accompanied by a gourd-like vessel and a small shallow dish with three legs upon which it rested. One time containers, no doubt, of food and drink.

Again the floor sounded hollow, and yet a third grave was found beneath the upper two. To make the long story short, again and yet again was this condition repeated until the total of five rich graves was recorded. The contents included a wealth of pottery, copper bells, incense, rock-crystal beads, and jade. This was unprecedented for that graveless city, and Thompson greatly rejoiced.

By this time the ground level upon which the pyramid had been built was reached, and he was expecting nothing further. So you may imagine his surprise when a steel bar accidentally dropped upon the floor gave forth the same resonant clang that he had learned signified "Good-sized cavity below!"

With great difficulty the heavy stone floor was raised, but this time, instead of a grave, he encountered a flight of steps hewn out of the solid rock.

This was mystery indeed, even for mysterious Chichen Itza! I really believe that of all exciting and tantalizing things in the world a hidden flight of steps penetrating living rock receives undisputed first prize.

They were choked with ashes and dust so finely pulverized that it was a smothering task in that airless pit to try to clean them sufficiently for passage. Baskets were filled and passed by a series of hands to the top where the débris was sorted for any specimens of interest.

Finally the steps were clear, and seemed to Thompson's great disappointment to lead exactly nowhere. Solid rock walls closed in the pointless little staircase without apparent crack or opening. But once more the place was sounded with the steel bar, and from the floor came again the deep hollow note which spoke so much more truly than human eyes.

Minute inspection with a candle showed a slab so cunningly fitted that it had completely escaped notice before. It was pried back and a long screaming blast of icy air rushed up from below the men's feet, putting out the candles and chilling the overheated bodies of the workers. For the brief second before the lights failed, they had glimpsed an enormous pitch-black hole, so thoroughly terrible in appearance as to complete the freezing of the blood begun by the swirling cold air.

The two assisting natives were stricken by terror into a paralyzed silence—then through chattering teeth one of them stuttered, "T-t-truly it is the mouth of hell." Thompson told me that he was left poised over the brink, poorly balanced and afraid to move a finger in the darkness for fear he would slip completely through. He sorely needed cool-headed help, and in order to puncture the "hell" idea as rapidly as possible, it was much to his interest to deliver a little lecture on orthodox Christian theology, putting due emphasis on fire and brimstone. He said he must have been both eloquent and convincing, for the Mayas recovered their wits and courage sufficiently to drag him back to safety.

By that time the air currents had adjusted themselves so the lights could be kindled again. And then his story goes on to describe how he descended by a rope into that inky darkness full fifty feet below the level of the ground, how he discovered the rock chamber to be a natural vault lying hidden below the earth's surface, how he found therein an altar strewn with sacred paraphernalia, and how all of this material was finally hoisted to the light of day.

The chief treasure was a lovely large vase of clear alabaster elaborately engraved with a meandering leaf design and filled to the brim with carved jade and pearls. Besides this there were votive urns nearly three feet high, surmounted by masks of a god, and there were beautiful crook-shaped flints.

Such altar equipment surpassed anything ever found in America. Surely they were the relics of a great priest who on the day of his passing decreed that his holy of holies should be forevermore hidden from sight of men. The secret of the entrance was sealed with the slab and his own body laid in the shaft above as perpetual guard over his treasures. And who knows but that the four graves above him were of lesser priests who represented some sinister sacrifice consummated in order further to guard the secret, or to accompany the Great One on his journey into the shadows?

Thoughts such as these caused Thompson to name the temple with its secret shaft the High Priest's Grave.

One Sunday morning the Chichen Itza archeological staff with concerted action moved upon the High Priest's Grave. We wanted to go and see for ourselves. Sunday mornings appeared to adapt themselves excellently to expeditions of all kinds. To begin with, the rising bell would awaken us at the luxurious hour of six instead of five, to a feeling languorously carefree. For fear this hour of rising appears unduly strenuous, let me explain that the cool of the early morning was a thing none of the workers wanted to sacrifice, for by eight o'clock the sun was searing the country with a torrid heat that made life move both slowly and with difficulty.

A leisurely breakfast was followed by an hour or two of comfortable laziness, which, however, began to get monotonous after a bit. One of us would begin to show evidence of a certain restlessness; another would be affected by the contagion, until we were all ready to follow the first person who said, "Let's go . . ."

On this particular day inspiration prompted one of us to suggest, "Let's go down the High Priest's Grave."

Juan was summoned as was customary, for as Oldest

Living Inhabitant, he was almost invariably consulted when matters of great moment were on foot. We pestered him with questions: "Were the stories of Thompson true? Was the stone shaft really forty feet deep? And was there a great natural cave beneath?"

"*Si, señores y señoras*, the stories are true. I myself was there."

"Good," we cried. "We want to go also."

"But why?" he asked. "The cave is now empty, and you already have heard how it is composed. The descent is very dangerous. Why do you trouble yourselves?"

As we really couldn't explain either in Spanish or English why we were insisting on troubling ourselves, we merely replied that we wanted to go, which after all was the whole of the truth.

Juan shrugged. He supposed he never would understand these gringos, and a wise man would waste no time trying. He disappeared and returned with his two stalwart sons and coils of rope. Isauro was a tall, beautifully proportioned boy, who on account of his remarkable intelligence had been of great assistance to us. But Remedios (think of naming a child "Remedies"!) was slow and fat and stupid, with the most charmingly good-natured disposition in the world (Fig. 11). He was faithful as an old dog and beloved by every one of us. Personally, I made up my mind that if anyone was going to hold my life on the end of a rope, I chose Remedios. There might be fine-drawn moments when both weight and constancy would be qualities of value!

We set out through the bush, arriving in due time at the High Priest's Temple. Clambering up its steep slopes, we came on the black shaft which yawned in the center of the floor. Then Juan unrolled his ropes. One long one there was, which he and the boys soon rigged over a stout pole lying across the hole. A little wooden board was lashed into place to serve as a seat "for the señoras," for the men were already clambering down the jutting stones fixed into the sides of the pit.

His other bundle, which Juan sent down ahead of him, consisted of a ladder with slight wooden rungs tied to rope sides. This, he explained, was for penetration to that deeper chamber below the pyramid. And he firmly stated that on that second descent men alone would go. It was no matter for ladies to attempt. I remember that I in particular scorned such a suggestion, with a rashness which I found later to be little short of idiotic.

Nina, who had come to Yucatan as Dr. Morley's secretary, took her place on the tiny wooden seat and was lowered slowly out of sight by Isauro and Remedios. After a time the tension slackened, the rope jerked in signal, and the seat was drawn up. (Fig. 33.)

My turn was next. As I slid into place, with a good grip on the rope, I exhorted the two to take great care, with a fluency in the foreign idiom I didn't know I possessed. The rope creaked and the descent began.

I found that the seat was very narrow and the rope inclined to twist. It was more than a little difficult to maintain an even keel, even using both feet and what hands I could spare to steady myself against the walls of the shaft. On the way up again I was to look on that precarious seat as a very throne of ease and safety in comparison with what lay behind me, but at the time my nerves were rather shaken. I reflected with some comfort on Juan's dictum against any farther penetration. My enthusiasm for secret caves was evaporating in an astonishing manner.

Finally my feet gratefully touched solid ground. I sent up the seat for the next comer and unhooked my flashlight. Sure enough, there were the steps cut into solid rock, even as the story had been told me. I crept cautiously down them, emerging into a tiny chamber wherein I could only crouch because the ceiling was so low. In its floor, indeed, taking up most of the available foot room, yawned a great hole. But what surprised me most of all was the fact that I was alone. Everybody, including Nina, had vanished. I was counting on her for moral support.

I turned the flashlight down the hole. The light followed the long, endless rope ladder, finally picking up the bottom and a small group of foreshortened men clustered at the ladder's foot. And with stark despair I saw Nina among them. She had deserted me, and in ignoring Juan's admonitions, she had put me in a dreadful quandary. For if the señorita had had the courage to descend that awful swinging ladder, it left no shred of moral cover for the señora to crouch behind. I knew I had to go, there was no way of honorable escape. Later, Nina told me that if I hadn't been so brash about it when we were discussing the matter safely above ground, she would never have gone herself! It was a good joke on both of us.

While I was hesitating before the grim job, someone else crawled into the chamber. It was Juan. I politely drew to one side and offered that he go first. I assured him that I was in no hurry—nor was I. Not the slightest! So I watched him as he wriggled through the narrow bottle-necked opening and began his climb down, eager to pick up details of technique.

Before he landed at the bottom I could hear yet another person begin to crawl down the steps. Somewhere above a stone was loosened, and hastily turning my light that way I was horrified to see a clattering boulder, accompanied by a shower of pebbles, come rattling down the steps. It was heading for the hole and I thought of Juan on the ladder directly in line below. It must have weighed about ten pounds, and was already traveling rapidly. By the time its speed was accelerated by the drop into space, it would be capable of dealing the unsuspecting Juan a wallop quite sufficient to break his skull.

I grabbed for it with my free left hand but so awkwardly that, although I stopped it, my fingers were badly mashed in the process. In the meantime the shower of dust and pebbles was arriving below to the great discomfort of everybody down there. They fled for cover, shouting uncomplimentary remarks at me, which, together with the bruise, so irritated my sense of heroic martyrdom that I was tempted to throw the boulder at them.

At any rate, these emotions were an excellent counter-irritant to my previous fear, so I immediately embarked upon the ladder and arrived safely at the bottom without once remembering what an excellent alibi for staying above my hurt hand would have provided me!

We had candles, but there were such a number of us crowded into the little secret room that we feared we might exhaust the air with their burning. So with flashlights we surveyed the ragged recesses of our surroundings. It was clear that the place was of natural formation shaped rather like a rough bottle with a tiny neck aperture at what was originally ground level. The builders of the old temple had cleverly placed it directly over this hole, and then, by piercing the heart of the pyramid with the stone shaft, had made it accessible as a very secret holy of holies.

The cave was empty when we found it, for Thompson had sifted every bit of dirt and dust there was in it for the jade and pearl treasure. One thing of interest we did note. At one side we could see what looked like the beginning of a natural passageway almost entirely blocked with huge stones fallen from the roof. Juan told us that tradition lingered among the "wilder" Mayas to the effect that this passage wound as a labyrinth underground for more than a mile, finally opening into a known fissure which led from the cliff wall bounding the Xtoloc Cenote.

We sat and chatted while time passed. Nobody seemed overly eager to tackle that ladder, so one pretext of delay followed another till we perceived the air to be growing noticeably stuffy. Gustav went up first and it appeared simple enough, but he fooled us. For his sailor training made light of rope ladders, and we were deceived by his appearance of ease as one is by a clever tight-rope walker. One after another the others left, and although the bottom of the ladder was held as firmly as possible, it swayed dreadfully, and the slow, careful progress of the climber spoke for itself. A few were even tactless enough to describe its horrors in graphic ejaculation, which operated powerfully against the morale of those waiting below.

My turn came. There is nothing much to say except that I did it. I am very poor at ladder climbing of even the more normal sort, and the conditions here were made no easier. The pitch darkness, wherein every shift of hand or foot had to be groped for, combined with the swaying, jerking instability to produce a sinking uncertainty in the pit of one's stomach, which has to be felt to be appreciated.

Pablo, the square little Maya chauffeur, had preceded me, and when I finally stepped out of the sling into the glorious daylight above, I found him sitting flat on the ground, his usual dark copper skin bleached to the tone of water-soaked liver. "Not for a hundred pesos would I do that again!" I heard him repeating over and over to himself and to anybody that would listen, but personally I thought that he put far too low a financial premium on the feat.

CHAPTER XVI

The Buried Temple

WITH the "day of rest" just described safely behind us, Monday morning brought again the old familiar routine.

The Temple of the Warriors appeared to be convalescing satisfactorily after its lengthy withdrawal from corporate existence. Day by day saw definite steps of achievement toward a condition of healthy renewal. The débris within was cleared away, the walls were restored to their original height, and the fallen columns in the building and in the Northwest Colonnade at its foot were set up in position. The stairway was completed, and the sides of the great pyramid face were rapidly being encased in their smooth white stone shell.

The latter proved to be much more ornate than usual for the steep pitch was made up of a series of four terraces of alternating sloping and perpendicular zones. The perpendicular zone forming narrow bands which completely encircled the pyramid was carved with hundreds of curious figures standing about two and a half feet high. There were reclining human figures, jaguars, eagles, and some curious creatures half bear and half coyote, each of which held a human heart in its claws.

The greater part of these long sculptured strips lay in disarticulated heaps at the pyramid's foot, and at first we despaired of ever separating them one from another, or of disentangling the sequence sufficiently to replace them in position. Guesswork is absolutely taboo in proper archeology. If the placement of each single element cannot be proved beyond all reasonable doubt, then a digger has no moral right ever to undertake any reconstruction. More harm has been done in the past by incorrect work of this kind than can be calculated, and such lessons painfully learned have made the modern schools of archeology cautious to the point of fanaticism. In Greece, late German, French, and Scandinavian archeologists have blithely built up missing fragments of sculpture out of their own imagination, reordering certain groups of figures according to their individual ideas of fitness, with results almost entirely German, French, or Scandinavian, and hardly Greek at all. A few of these errors have been detected and corrected, but such secondary work is always more difficult because a certain amount of valuable evidence is sure to have been destroyed in the meantime.

Therefore, although Earl thought he might possibly work out a fairly logical reconstitution of his thousand feet of sculptured banding, he was bound by the great unwritten law of accuracy to leave it undone even at the cost of detriment to the temple's appearance.

Then suddenly the key was laid at his hands—and by none other than the architect who had built the temple so many hundred years ago. For twice in the course of his planning the builder had changed his mind about the ultimate aspect of his temple, and on both those occasions he had covered over large sections of the sculptured band with solid masonry which kept it in place, so that it would not scale from the pyramid face and slip into ruin below. On the front, a narrow stair had been laid to the temple, and then, for some un-

known reason, the staircase was considerably broad-
ened, so that it extended over bits of sculptured band;
while at the corner, where the temple pyramid joined
the Court of the Thousand Columns, an even more
radical addition of a later hall built flush against the
sculptured band had preserved about three fourths of
the stones in order. Earl blessed the scatterbrained
builder who had deliberately wasted so much beautiful
carving, but who had in his carelessness made it possible for us to view long sections of all of the sculptured
strips in their original position. With those patterns it
was a comparatively simple matter to reassemble the
other stones and with an easy conscience restore them
to their places.

This emergency had been safely met, and while the
routine work went on of cleaning the rubble pyramid
faces to make a good backing for the masons to set up
the sculptured bands, Earl took time to draw a few deep
breaths. The season of 1926 was drawing to a close. It
was the second year of work on the Warriors' Temple,
and we all calculated that by the time the rains began
the thing would be done—and an impressive, clean-cut
architectural unit would stand resurrected from the
past.

On a Saturday afternoon, after the men had been
paid off, a few of us were visiting the temple and admir-
ing our handiwork. The tension of hurry was slacken-

Fig. 33

THE FIRST STAGE IN DESCENDING THE HIGH PRIEST'S GRAVE

After I had negotiated a forty-foot rope ladder which came at the foot of the stone well here shown, I looked upon this precarious little chair as a very throne of safety. Alma Reed, the famous newspaper correspondent, is steadying the ropes which I clasp so intensely.

Courtesy of Carnegie Institution

Fig. 34

THE UNEXPECTED COLUMN

When accidentally discovered this column revealed the presence of an earlier and more beautiful building buried beneath the Warriors' Temple.

ing, and our week-end was our own to enjoy as we
pleased, but like the bus man who takes his holiday by
going bus riding, we were drawn back to the spot as
by a magnet. We wandered around to the north side,
idly looking the place over, and I remember Earl remarked to Dr. Morley: "Well, now the Warriors' is so
nearly done, what will we tackle next?"

Truly the Maya gods must have laughed aloud to
hear him. The Plumed Serpent himself hovering over
his ancient home must have relaxed his rigid snarl to
smile a moment in derision before he loosened a tiny
pebble from the slope and rattled it down at Earl's feet.
We looked up to see whence it came and noticed a
great stump protruding from the pyramid; some careful native had that morning been undermining its base
preparatory to uprooting it. It was a gnarled old stump
clutching with frantic roots at its precarious hold, and
was very picturesque. Someone unslung a camera, saying, "That ought to make a good picture. Help me get
a set up, somebody," and clambered up the steep slope.
Earl followed, using the stump itself to hoist himself
the last yard or two. As he sought a foothold in the
cavity beneath it, he noticed a bit of carved stone
clasped between the roots. It stood vertically, as if
in position, but even then he thought it might be only
a detached bit of carving dragged in by the mason's
helpers as they might any ordinary bowlder. The pyramid was salted with such examples of sculpture, some

worthless, but a few had proved to be intrinsically beautiful and valuable in themselves. With his pocket knife he gouged out a bit more dirt, laying bare a strip of stone a few inches high, and then, burrowing deeper, he perceived that the carved block he had first seen rested upon another and that the two were firmly cemented together. He says now that when the portent of these two stones began to dawn on him, the hair at the back of his neck rose in a cold chill of apprehension and excitement, and that many times since he wished he had covered his find quietly and hastened to bury it forevermore behind the sheathing of the pyramid.

The first we knew of anything untoward was his hoarse command, "Bring me a pick." And then, with the activity of a squirrel excavating for some choice long-buried nut, he flew into the dirt beneath that stump, clinging with one hand as well as he could, while with shortened grip on the pick handle he tore away dirt and rubble. The top of a square column emerged, then stone below stone, until at a depth of seven feet a red polished floor appeared. (Fig. 34.)

It was plain now that in our two long years we had been working only on the frosting to our cake, while all the time there was buried in the pyramid's heart an older building. I imagine that the Plumed Serpent must have given a triumphant lash of his tail before he settled down to another two years of contented apathy, waiting for a conscientious archeologist to follow out the new clue which was to result in even further glorification of his temple.

For a while we had no way of knowing whether much of the older building was buried in the pyramid or whether only the single tell-tale column emerging near the corner remained to trick us into our high hopes. Obviously the thing to do was to trace the line of the floor along the pyramid faces until its boundaries were reached. It was dangerous work, for the platform upon which the Warriors' Temple was built was high above the new column's face, and on the north side this platform was so narrow that much undercutting would carry one beneath the none-too-secure massive temple walls.

Earl clung to a rope which he fixed to a series of stumps and worked along the line of the floor toward the east, laying bare its broken edge. Finally the floor line stopped sharply and a few inches farther a series of plaster-covered blocks sloped sharply downward. This boded well for it appeared that one limit of the buried structure had been reached, and that it had been comprised of some kind of a colonnaded hall built upon a pyramided base even as was the greater Temple of the Warriors.

Thence, returning to the original corner, he burrowed into the west face of the pyramid where presumably the crest of a second column stood. It was there. Then a third was found, and finally the stub of an upright wall. Thus the size of our building was established. It apparently measured about fifty feet square, and with rueful heart Earl realized that the major portion of it lay directly under the Temple of the Warriors.

For a time he seriously debated whether or not it would be worth while to go to the terrific effort and expense necessary to clean this second temple without harming the beautiful building above. The new structure seemed to be nothing but a rather exact replica of the later one, although built on a much smaller scale, and it was questionable whether one would be justified in working it in spite of the interest of its position.

Then an unexpected discovery set all his doubts at rest, for one morning Manuel raised an excited shout from the little platform he had dug for himself before one of the column faces. Earl hurried up the slope to find the man staring fascinated at a block of stone emerging from the rubble at his feet. It was one of the most magnificently colored things either of them had ever laid eyes on—all hues of the rainbow intensified a hundredfold.

"Oh, Engineer, what is it?" breathed Manuel.

As Earl recovered from a paralysis of astonishment at finding such an object where only dirt and stone were to be expected, he snatched Manuel's shovel and in a few moments laid bare a serpent's head—a yard square, much like those found the previous year, but infinitely more richly colored. Close by it was another, and then came a series of blocks made from the fallen jamb of door, glorious in color as the day they were new.

"By the Great Plumed Serpent himself!" ejaculated Earl. "This place is a treasure house. Manuel, go brush clear a little space on the wall where we found that projecting stub, and tell me what you find."

Manuel worked carefully a few moments with the trowel, then shouted, "Color, Engineer—like those others—only more color."

That settled it. The Buried Temple would have to be excavated. From the rain-washed stones above, we thought we had found adequate pictures of an original Maya temple, but this place, which had been purposely covered while still fresh, revealed their true state to have been magnificent beyond anyone's previous conjectures.

The tale of the next two years, if adequately told, would fill a book in itself. Only Earl himself could do justice to the infinite amount of planning and careful work in which this Buried Temple involved him.

The first morning of his third season he called Juan to him. "To-day we start excavating the building beneath this platform. I want a quadrilla of your best men." The old *mayordomo* looked up at the great wall of the Warriors' Temple, then over the brink to the columns below, and, his face clearing of an evident puzzlement, replied, "*Si, si, Ingeniero*, you wish the corner of the big temple taken down. *Bueno*, I will find paint to mark and number each stone so that later we can build it back almost as it is now—that is, if you think it possible to ever put it back, when its resting place is cut away."

"No, Juan, I am not going to take these walls down."

"Then you will not dig beneath them?"

"But surely, did I not just say I would? In the end, the Buried Temple is going to stand as clean and empty as a cellar beneath the one above, but not one stone of this masonry is going to be moved."

Juan looked aghast. A hundred questions crowded one another in his puzzled eyes—then, remembering his code of civility and at the same time a few impossible things he had already seen performed, he answered most politely, "*Muy bien, Ingeniero.*"

It was an anxious year before Earl made good his word, but at the end of that period his prophecy was fulfilled—the Buried Temple stood clean and empty, completely encased within the Warriors' pyramid, and not a stone of the fearful bulk overhead had budged from its position. The details of engineering which went into the achievement of that end will necessarily be condensed, but I hope that will not seriously detract from an appreciation of the splendid feat it was.

The first phase involved a concrete foundation beneath the long stretches of temple walls which were to be undermined. This base was reinforced with steel beams which had to cross one another at the corner. The walls were so weakened and crumbling with age that the process had to be undertaken a tiny bit at a time with infinite care that some keystone was not jarred from place, bringing the whole thing down about the workers' ears.

Henry Roberts had been signed on that year to serve an apprenticeship in Yucatan field work. He had been working at the theoretical end of Maya archeology at Harvard, and was intent on furthering his education about the Maya. When Earl confronted him with the monstrous problem in hand he swung into the idea forthwith, and from beginning to end proved of inestimable value in working out the multiplicity of practical details which cropped up from time to time.

Gustav throve on difficult jobs, and he probably never had met with one more ticklish than the construction of the series of wooden forms through which the concrete was poured, for each had to be provided with inner channels for the insertion of steel beams after the first pouring of concrete had set, and a deviation of a fraction of an inch in their construction would prevent a free movement of the long steel bars when they had to be slipped into place. It involved an enormous amount of arithmetic, of course; one day, when I came upon him as he was poring over a ten-foot board almost completely covered with tiny figures, I stopped to ask,

"Gustav, are you working on the Maya calendar, or calculating the national debt of Norway?" Quick as a wink he answered, "No, ma'am, I was just checking up on Einstein, because if it's true that parallel lines meet, then I'm out of luck." He indicated a wooden complexity beside him which looked like a model for the Eiffel Tower, and explained that it was the framework for the concrete block beneath the temple corner. With its sides and bases and six inner channels in two planes to permit the two sets of three steel beams to cross each other within the cube, I didn't wonder that he required a ten-foot plank twelve inches wide on which to do his figuring, and said so. "As you say in America," he replied with a twinkle, "this is less than the half of it. I don't waste any pages in my pocket notebook." With a twist of his hand, he flipped the board over, and I saw that the other side was covered also.

When the cement foundation for the Warriors' was completed the next step involved its support from below. A schematic plan of the Buried Temple, when drawn out on cross-section paper, indicated where the columns still hidden should be standing. One of them was calculated to be almost directly under the Warriors' west wall, and one under the corner. Earl saw how he could use this to his advantage, so he set men to excavating a straight-sided narrow pit in search of the crest of the latter. About eight feet down it was found, and by utilizing it he saved fully half of the height of the supporting column he was going to cast. Forms were built on top of it, reaching up to the temple foundation, and a reinforced concrete pillar soon was planted which, together with the old stone shaft, made a firm resting place for the mass of wall above. This process was repeated for the stone column under the west wall, then two additional full-length sixteen-foot pillars were cast as additional support. As each one was completed we breathed a little more easily, for it meant just that much sturdier bracing of the mass above.

Then the real test came, for slowly the supporting earth was dug away between the pillars, and bit by bit, as the Buried Temple was emptied, even more completely the weight of the upper building was transferred to its artificial braces.

Finally only a single strategic block of rubble lay in place—with its removal, the practical result of all Earl's plans would be finally decided. If his calculations were erroneous the catastrophe would prove beyond accounting, for a full quarter of the upper temple would be precipitated into the lower, ruining them both beyond all help, with fatal results to the workers. When the day came Earl cleared the buildings of all the men and descended to do the work alone. Every one of us protested fiercely, but he was adamant. "No, the plan is mine, and if it fails I cannot hold myself responsible for the lives of those who trust me."

We stood on the outside listening for the sound of his pick. Again and again the blows reverberated from the pyramid's hollow heart. We knew his scheme was to undermine the fill, and then to let the whole mass down at once. After what seemed an interminable interval, a final sharp blow was succeeded by dead silence, then the trickle of smaller stones, and at last a great crashing boom as the body of the rubble fell away from beneath the upper walls. We fastened our eyes on the great Warriors' Temple—not a stone moved, not a seam opened. The plan had succeeded, for the temple stood as firmly on its artificial legs as it ever had on its old foundations. When Earl appeared, with a broad smile replacing the white strained look of the morning, we shouted in triumph, and the little brown workers cheered and cheered as if they would never stop.

The color promised by the first probing of the Buried Temple was amplified beyond all measure. Every column was glitteringly brilliant as the day it was new, and the walls, which were in perfect shape, bore great writhing serpents stretched in rhythmic coils across their faces (Fig. 36).

Long before the work just described was completed, Jean and I moved in with our painting materials, and taking up positions wherever we could find them, so as to be out from under the excavators' feet, we hastened to copy the beautiful patterns before they should dry and fade a particle. This new work of ours proved to be more than we could handle together, so Jean sent for a painter he had known in Mexico to come and assist us. Lowell Hauser came in time to be a valuable find. He not only possessed the painstaking accuracy necessary for that kind of copying, but he succeeded in maintaining the most remarkable poise in the very midst of the constant dog fight that went on between Jean and myself. Lowell's work, which is very successful, completely shears the artistic temperament myth of its sharp teeth. Try as we could, neither Jean nor I succeeded in embroiling him in battle, and I regret to say that, although we admired his splendid example in a detached fashion, we never brought ourselves to the point of copying it.

The sanctuary of the Buried Temple, with the exception of painted walls and colored sculptured columns, was quite bare. When the builders of the Warriors' pyramid had decided to fill up the smaller building, in order to incorporate it as a solid masonry block in their structure, they had evidently cleared that room of the altar and the two great benches which lined the walls. Bare unpainted plaster showed where these things had originally stood, and it was with the greatest regret that we realized we could never know what they had looked like. In a temple so magnificent they could not help but be very beautiful themselves.

In the meantime, the men had been clearing around

the outer faces of the buried pyramid by driving passages into the enclosing débris in such a manner that the narrow tunnels would eventually completely encircle the outside of the building. Earl put in charge of this work Angelino, the head mason, whose efficient craftsmanship and snub-nosed old face, that somehow looked Irish, quite belied the name of "Little Angel" bestowed by his parents.

One day Angelino brought to light a richly painted stone much like those found in the Warriors' Temple but even more brilliant and beautiful. For a time similar blocks cropped up sporadically, and we thought that they were only evidence of the casual manner in which the old builders had torn up ancient walls to provide rubble filling for raising the great pyramids. But when they began to come from the débris so thickly that it took Angelino's helpers all their time to bring the blocks to me for inspection, it suddenly dawned on me that I might have enough to attempt some of that fitting together which had proved so successful before.

Gradually a line of gorgeously adorned human beings began to take form on the floor of the Buried Temple where I had laid them out. They were so well preserved that it wasn't very difficult to do such reassembling, and the results were good enough to be positively thrilling. Curiously enough, they shaped themselves in long narrow lines only three stones deep instead of in great rectangular panels such as were customary. Blue border lines showed this pattern to be the complete one, and I was very puzzled as to where they might have been placed originally. Day by day they kept coming, and I laid them so that they almost completely encircled the sanctuary; still the obvious solution never occurred to me. The shade of the old Plumed Serpent must have writhed in anguish every time he heard me say, "Now where do you suppose these stones came from before they were chucked into the fill outside this sanctuary?" Then one afternoon, while I sat back to rest a moment from my labors, I happened to glance at the edge of the raw white plaster at the back of where one of the benches had stood, and my eye idly noted some splashings of blue paint spilled over onto the black background. I remarked carelessly to Lowell, "I wonder where that bench has disappeared. I see it must have been rimmed in blue." Then something whispered within me: "Blue, Ann, *blue!*" I stared at my blue-rimmed line of stones laid on the floor, shouted, "Lowell, give me that tape measure instantly!"

Of course you have guessed far more quickly than I in my colossal stupidity that my line of stones was the bench, and that all the time I was doing my futile wondering I was laying them almost precisely in the place they belonged.

When this fact had been completely proved, Earl became most interested in the whereabouts of the lost altar. Since the elements of the benches were stowed away so close at hand in the new pyramid, he hoped desperately that the altar parts would be found near by, but the most assiduous searching revealed nothing. A careful cleaning of the floor had showed that shallow sockets had been gouged at regular intervals in the red plaster. Evidently the altar had been of the Atlantean type—that is, supported on small stone human figures, like the one upstairs. But nary an Atlantean nor a stone-top slab could be found.

He was taking notes on the subject—calculating the probable dimensions and number of supporting figures as well as he could—while I was painting a copy of the South bench. Then he too was visited with sudden inspiration.

"Ann, you have just finished painting that altar upstairs—how high is it?"

"Two feet six inches," I answered. That was an easy question, for in reducing the dimensions to the small scale of my painted reproductions, I had probably measured the thing at least seventy-five times.

Earl laid the tape against the evident mark on the temple wall where the lost altar had stood, then shook his head. "No, that's nine inches short. I thought for a minute that—— I say, how much of their feet was buried under the floor?"

"Nine inches," I abstractedly replied, for I was trying hard to get the proper effect where the red floor paint had splattered and dirtied the lower edges of my bench's blue rim.

But still he persisted, "Well, how much is two feet six inches plus nine inches?"

I laid aside my brush with exasperation. "Thirty-nine inches, and am I a painter or an adding machine?"

But he was dangling a tape measure gleefully in front of my nose with his finger on the thirty-nine-inch mark. "Just the height of the lost altar. That's where it is. They carried it upstairs, and since it was nine inches too high the stone workers buried the feet." And thus were solved the two mysteries of the Missing Altar and the Buried Feet on one lucky day.

When the last stroke of work was completed, Earl closed and locked the heavy door of the Buried Temple in relief. A perilous piece of excavation was safely behind him, and the dim hollow vaults of the empty temple had given up an artistic wealth of mural painting and sculpture exceeding anything ever before found in America. The rooms were bare and clean as brush and broom could make them. Nor then did he dream that the greatest treasure still lay in the empty sanctuary—a treasure which would overshadow anything he had found before.

This time the old Plumed Serpent must have lain quiet as a mouse, fearing lest the most precious jewel of all be taken from him. He was satisfied, for with the exception of muffled blows still sounding in the pyramid's heart where the masons were completing their underground passages, the two buildings had been restored to him in all their first splendor. His need for us had passed, and fiercely he hoped that his secret might never be found. There had been days of keen apprehension when a dozen men had passed and repassed near its hiding place, so close that less than two inches of earth intervened between heavy boots and the hidden horde. But at last, presumably, he was nearly rid of us, and he thought us stupid dolts indeed to have let slip this greatest thing of all.

Fig. 35

THE SHEATHING OF THE PYRAMID WENT FORWARD

Meanwhile, our workmen, like industrious ants, burrowed behind the walls of stone into the heart of the mound, clearing the temple buried therein.

Fig. 36

IN THE DIM VAULTS OF THE BURIED TEMPLE

Richly painted walls, carved and colored columns, and smooth, exquisite sculpture gleamed like jewels.

CHAPTER XVII

Altar Treasure

DEDICATION day was near at hand. The temple was just about ready to be turned over formally to the Mexican government. Various high officials were on their way from Mexico City to attend the ceremony, and Dr. Merriam and Dr. Kidder had come from Washington to officiate at the presentation. Mexico is very proud of its old monuments and devotes a deal of expense and attention to those found in its territory. In this respect she sets an excellent example to other nations for she contributes from her annual national budget more money for archeological exploration and preservation than any other country in the world.

The entire Chichen Itza staff was busy as a swarm of bees in preparation for the event. Every nook and cranny was swept and garnished with the utmost care and solicitude. And in addition, since the end of the dry season was drawing nigh, we were hastening with our own individual work in order to catch up all the loose ends before it was necessary to return to the United States.

Old Angelino was burrowing his last tunnel through the Warriors' pyramid, the one which was to prove conclusively that yet other buildings had not been buried in its far corners. By this time he was an expert at the dangerous task, so Earl felt free for the first time to devote himself to checking up on a little private idea of his own. This particular hunch, by the way, was to produce such remarkable eleventh-hour results that people have often asked him just where and how the inspiration happened to strike him. In his own words, the story runs somewhat as follows:

"One evening last winter [1927] during the Annual

Exhibition held in the Carnegie Institution at Washington, D. C., I was on duty to explain to the visitors the Chichen Itza exhibit which had been installed. During a quiet interval my thoughts drifted away from the Maya city, back to the ancient ruins in New Mexico where I had spent my boyhood. For some reason I began thinking of the dedication offerings of turquoise and shell, which I had found built into the sacred rooms there. Then, like a bolt from the blue, it struck me that maybe the Maya had done the same thing." In so many instances have the peoples of old America given evidence of thinking and acting in similar manner, even when they were thousands of miles separated, that a parallel in the present case was just possible. "I remember thinking then that the altars would be the most logical places to bury such offerings, and I determined to test out the possibility when I returned to Yucatan."

However, when he did return, the press of immediate tasks demanded his attention, and in the difficult work involved by the roofing of the Buried Temple and tunneling around its base there was no time for the chase of a phantasy until close on the season's end. When Dr. Merriam arrived, Earl told him of his idea about the altars, and he was instantly and intensely interested.

The two of them set out together one morning, fairly exuding secretiveness, while brown-skinned Danyel, who was a most careful digger, was ordered to fall in behind.

First they went to the sculptured altar in the Northwest Colonnade, and when the protective sand had been swept from its polished red surface a large white patch was seen to mar its beauty. Dr. Merriam looked at Earl, and Earl stared back in dismay.

"It looks as if someone had been here before us, but it also seems as if there might be something to the idea, doesn't it? Start in here, Danyel, and we'll see."

Beneath the white plaster coat, the altar body showed distinct evidence of having been stirred, for bits of the red floor were scattered throughout. Against the foot of the back wall a broken pottery urn was found, but nothing else. It was quite evident that the place had been looted of some objects of value; then the thieves, for some unknown reason, had neatly refilled the hole, plastered it over, but had not repainted it red. I never have figured out why they should have taken such pains to cover the traces of their crime and then neglected the most obvious step of all, unless it was that they were caught at the task. If that was true, the booty must have been hijacked, because it certainly was not restored to its rightful position.

Next, Earl and Dr. Merriam turned to the altar in the North Colonnade, this time very hopefully, because in spite of early bad luck the very fact that an offering had once been there was most encouraging. The center of the second altar was gouged into with no success, the trench carried to the back wall, but still nothing was found, and Danyel, who had become infected with the excitement of the chase, leaned dejectedly against his pick. Suddenly he brightened.

"Engineer, there is another altar of solid stone where you and I worked the first year. Maybe that one will not deceive us so."

"*Bueno, Danyel, vamanos!*" And the three treasure seekers, probably mindful of the old adage that the grass in the next field is always greener, moved on.

This time, the very first blow of the pick sounded against a flat slab that rang hollow. Trowels were used, and when the great stone was lifted a sizable cavity was revealed, but seemingly empty except for a little fine dust over the floor. Earl sifted the dust carefully between his fingers, and in the very last corner discovered a small pottery dish, two dishes of shell, and a few badly decayed bones of a small bird. Obviously the carefully constructed vault had been made to hold something of more value than these few wretched specimens. Doubtless the objects of real beauty had been wrought in some perishable substance—carved wood or richly woven tapestry—which had perished through decay.

"Well," said Earl, "we haven't contributed in a very startling fashion to Maya archeology so far. Let's go back and tackle that second altar again. It can't be absolutely bare. If there is anything there, we'll get it if we have to dig the whole heart out."

Danyel flew at the masonry like an ambitious gopher until Earl put a restraining hand on his shovel handle. "Just a minute, my friend. You mustn't throw jade around the country like that." And to Danyel's intense chagrin he stooped and rescued from the pile of débris a brilliant green bead as large as a walnut.

They all combed with their fingers through the dirt that had been thrown out, but evidently that bit of jade was the only object which had been in danger of being lost. Then, carefully working the bottom of the pit, ten more small pieces of the green stone were found, a few bits of shell, and two large disks made of a soft yellow sandstone.

Affairs seemed to be improving, but the last solid altar had been tapped, and the finds had been admittedly scanty. Earl was disappointed, and he felt hardly toward the long-treasured hunch which seemed to have let him down so badly. Just then the noon bell rang and he and Danyel plodded dejectedly for the Buried Temple in order to lock up their tools, while Dr. Merriam returned to the hacienda.

In the Buried Temple, Earl looked speculatively at the spot where the altar had once stood. Since this one had not been of the solid masonry type, but had consisted of slabs supported by little stone human figures, any chance of offerings seemed remote. The only possible opportunity would lie in its burial beneath the floor.

Earl took Danyel's pick and tapped over the entire area once covered by the altar in an effort to detect the tell-tale resonant ring betraying a hidden cavity. No spot sounded conclusively hollow, but one point seemed to echo a bit more than the rest. Beneath it Danyel dug, but he encountered nothing but stones laid in lime. The cavity was only a tiny hollow where the mortar had not completely filled the space beneath a stone chip.

"It's no good, Danyel. You go get your lunch, for you have worked well. My luck is bad, that's all."

Earl stood there alone for a space to adjust himself to the disappointment, for he found that he had hoped for far more than he had ever realized in his speculations on the idea. I believe then the spirit of the old Plumed Serpent must have fairly held its phantom breath in fear of this intrusive alien white man who at that very moment stood within a hand's breadth of the treasure it must have wished to guard for itself.

Just then Jean and Gustav came down into the temple to leave the tools of their various crafts over the noon hour. Earl told them about what he had been up to all morning and how poorly it had turned out. "Well, sor," said the loyal Norwegian, "if you can't find anything, then there's nothing to find."

Maybe it was that remark that tipped the scale, possibly it was a characteristic dogged persistence that wouldn't admit defeat, or again, it might have been a

certain brooding, intangible sense of old memories
that hung over the spot which chimed in with the earnest seeker's tautly strung mind. At any rate, as the two
boys tell it, Earl suddenly shook himself and said,
"Wait a minute, fellows, I want to tap this floor once
more." Carefully he sounded the area again and again
while they all listened with rapt attentiveness. It was as
if all the senses were for the moment paralyzed, while
their several powers were concentrated in hearing alone.

Finally, between the hole that Danyel had dug
and the back wall, a spot no larger than a saucer
seemed to give forth a deeper rumble. One blow with
the pick point, and the blade broke through to pass
into a cavity below. Bare hands clawed at the bits
of broken floor crust and, thrusting his fingers in the
hole made by the pick, Earl raised a lid of stone. Three
heads craned eagerly over the opening to peer down into
a cylindrical recess of polished stone. From the bottom
came a gleam of jade and something that even in the
half light of the gloomy temple glinted as blue as a bit
of tropical sky.

"Careful, boys." Earl's voice shook. "We'll have to
go slowly here, for we've got something real at last."

They covered the opening with Jean's drawing board,
and carefully tested the padlock on the barred temple
door.

At their slightly belated lunch the three conspirators
kept their eyes strictly on their plates and ate so little

withal—an abstinence very contrary to custom—that their elaborately circumspect manner fairly shrieked of the extraordinary. Finally, Dr. Morley—I think it was he—couldn't bear it another minute.

"Look here, old man, the proverbial cat that ate the oft-mentioned canary must have had an expression precisely like yours. What *have* you found?"

Earl swallowed the greater part of a whole boiled potato at one gulp and replied, "If you want to learn something to your advantage, meet me at the Buried Temple at two o'clock."

On the dot of time the entire personnel of Chichen gathered before the door of the Temple and stared in at the familiar empty interior, which, now that the hole in the floor was covered by the big drawing board, seemed to offer no clue whatever as to where the mystery lay. When Earl came down the steps and teasingly displayed a flashlight, a teaspoon, and a camel's-hair brush, anticipation grew as keen as it was puzzled.

First he lengthened the hole that Danyel had dug earlier in the day in order that his working position might not be so awkward. Then the drawing board was carefully laid aside and a score or so of quickly drawn breaths, as we all crowded in, attested to everybody's startled interest.

At the center of the cavity lay a large spherical ball of dark jade polished as glass. This was one of the *zaz-tuns* or "light stones" which the old priests had used for prophecy, much as do the crystal gazers of the Orient to-day. Beside it was a piece of apple-green jade beautifully carved to represent a human face, and flanking it were two more jade beads and strings of shell. Near these were some bird bones.

These things could be detected by the glow of the flashlight but beneath them lay a film of dust which had filtered in during the long ages while the jar remained buried in the earth.

Then Earl reached for a long-handled camel's-hair brush which I recognized with some dismay as the last one in my possession from which the insects had not devoured the bristles. Delicately brushing toward one side, the fourth or fifth stroke left behind it a broad swath of blue so intense and beautiful that we cried out in astonishment.

Dr. Morley fetched Earl a whacking blow on the shoulders. "Old man, it's a turquoise mosaic. They are as rare as hen's teeth. Hurry up and see how big it is!"

He was right, but hurry was impossible, much as Earl's fingers itched to reveal the treasure immediately. The measure that differentiates archeology from the pell-mell joy of treasure seeking seems to lie chiefly in the science of delay, which brings acutest mental torture to its followers. Great age inevitably makes exceedingly fragile the majority of archeological finds, so that the utmost care has to be used in dealing with them. In addition to this, photographic records have to be made every step of the way when anything is being uncovered.

A camera was set up, and a hasty group calculation concerning the light in the sanctuary determined a three-minute exposure. When the first film was taken, it was rushed to the laboratory to be developed, and was found to be completely blank. The time was doubled, and still the film showed no record. Mirrors were rigged for reflecting purposes, and fifteen minutes were accorded the stubborn camera. Still not the slightest vestige of anything appeared upon the film. I began to wonder if the thing was real, for it seemed disconcertingly like one of those illusions which a cold-blooded camera's eye refuses to see. Finally, in exasperation, Earl opened the shutter, resolutely turned his back on it, and stared at the opposite wall for thirty-seven endless minutes. I don't know what dictated such an interval, except that possibly it was as long as he could bear the suspense. At its termination he snapped out the plate holder and handed it to the messenger, saying, "If this one isn't any good I'm going to resign and give the job to somebody without any nerves."

The last exposure proved to be timed to a second—for the picture was perfect. But not until then could he proceed to uncover further the precious turquoise mosaic. As he swept it clearer of the heavy dust film, which was scooped out with the teaspoon, he found that it covered the whole bottom of the container—indeed, it fitted so accurately that we later decided the heavy stone jar must have been made precisely for the purpose of holding it.

But now it began to be apparent that the problem of clearing the disk and of successfully getting it out of its deep snug bed was going to be terrifically difficult. The mosaic had been encrusted on a slab of wood which had rotted away into powder from behind it, and the only thing which held it together at all was a thin film of the adhesive which had originally fastened it to the wooden backing. Although most of the pattern was intact, nevertheless the slightest jar or a heavy breath would shatter it hopelessly into a meaningless chaos.

The situation was truly precarious. Earl says he felt like a dog that has found a porcupine. He didn't dare touch the mosaic and he couldn't leave it alone. Everybody went into executive session to determine what to do, and many were the schemes that were suggested and rejected as impracticable. You may imagine we kept at a safe distance from the treasure, and we tiptoed lest we jar the floor. Earl shivered at his strenuous soundings with the heavy pick in the morning, and was fairly appalled when he remembered the débris he had crashed to the ground when the temple was being cleared. The top of the jar was not more than three inches beneath the floor, where solid tons of stone and rubble had rumbled in their fall.

Finally it was determined to strengthen the disk as much as possible where it lay. A thin solution of Ambroid—a strong waterproof glue—was spread over the surface, a very little at a time lest the ether-like solvent soften the original adhesive before it evaporated. After half-a-dozen coats had been applied, the surface appeared considerably stronger.

By that time night had fallen, and as a thoughtless member of the party had remarked in Spanish to some natives that twenty thousand dollars in American gold would be small value for the mosaic, we were a bit apprehensive. Gustav and Rogers volunteered for all-night guard duty. They relieved each other during the dinner hour, then camped for the night inside the barred door, armed and ready for a defense which fortunately proved unnecessary.

The next morning the problem arose of removing the disk, jar, and all to safer keeping at the hacienda. First the jar had to be freed from the solid ground wherein it was snugly imbedded without allowing a single grain to fall inside. In order to cover the aperture satisfactorily, two heavy wires were cut slightly larger than the diameter of the jar. These were bent until they could be admitted into the opening and then sprung so that their ends pressed firmly against the slightly rough stone. Upon these supporting crossbars, set at right angles to one another, was laid a disk of paper upturned at the edges. Then the crack between stone and paper

was closed by the drip of a tallow candle, thus completely sealing the open top (Figs. 38 and 39).

With the greatest possible care the earth was cleared
from around the jar in such a manner that not the
slightest vibration or shock would be transmitted to the
container. Again a photograph was taken of jar and lid
in position, then with painful solicitude the find was
lifted from its age-old nest and set upon a short plank.
About board and stone Gustav wove a mesh of heavy
ropes, knotted as only a sailor knows how, and made a
sling which passed over a stout pole. With Gustav at
one end of the pole and Earl at the other, it was lifted
slowly to their shoulders, and while Jean and Dr. Morley held it to prevent any side swing, the four proceeded
with cautious slow steps to the top of the Warriors'
pyramid, down the steep staircase to the ground, and
over the long rough mile to the hacienda (Fig. 37). Mr.
and Mrs. Walter Trumbull, who were visiting Chichen at
the time, took some moving pictures of the careful
progress, and they said that they'd have to speed it up
in the projector or people would think that they were
giving them "slow-motion" pictures. When the paper
cover was removed, as far as anybody could judge not a
sliver of turquoise had been displaced.

Obviously, however, the disk could never be moved
from Chichen, and it would perish if left in its original
state. It had to be replaced upon a new base of strong
wood without too much delay. Dr. Merriam cabled to

New York, requisitioning the services of a phenomenally skillful Japanese artist preparator who was then working for the American Museum of Natural History.

Mr. Shiochi Ichikawa luckily caught an immediate boat and within a week's time he appeared at Chichen, vastly concerned because someone had told him we lived on lizards and snakes. For a day or two he haunted the kitchen before meal time, but finally he was reassured as to our diet of turkey and good American corned beef, which latter nourishment, by rights, ought to have bothered him more than it seemed to.

Under Mr. Ichikawa's deft hands the disk was rapidly glued to a smooth round wooden plaque backing. Some of it was solid enough to be moved in sections from the deep jar. Other bits had decayed so badly that they had to be transferred a stone at a time. When we found by actual count that more than three thousand separately cut mosaic turquoises had been utilized in its composition the magnitude of the task of repair seemed appalling. And even more than before, we felt respect for those ancient jewelers who so accurately shaped and ground to an almost paper thinness the infinity of tiny sections which made up their desired pattern.

The plaque was more than a simple jeweled studding which filled a round wooden surface. An intricate design in different shades of color had been worked out with the greatest care, using stones of varying sizes so shaped as to outline the patterns to be accented.

At the center of the plaque was a disk of soft pinkish sandstone about two and one-half inches in diameter. This was encrusted with mosaic plates of an iron oxide. The use of such an ugly low-grade rock in the very center of a priceless jewel is rather puzzling. Sandstone is soft and crumbly, would never have taken a high polish, and is of no intrinsic value whatsoever. However, for some reason the Mayas held it in high regard, and used it almost invariably in dedicatory offerings. The same material composed the two disks which were found in the North Colonnade altar and the two disks found beneath the front corner stones of the Temple of the Warriors. In the turquoise plaque the same custom held, and though this time the unsightly sandstone was hidden from view, nevertheless, the offering was carefully endowed with its peculiar powers or properties. Perhaps it was derived from some sacred mountain far from Yucatan, or it may have been a part of a mother altar in an earlier home—but that is yet purely a matter for conjecture.

Encircling the sandstone center was a narrow ring of infinitesimally tiny brilliant blue turquoises. From this radiated strips of a yellow vegetable material which divided the main part of the plaque into eight wedge-shaped segments. Each alternate one of the eight was of plain turquoise mosaic, while the remaining four bore a pattern consisting of the head and claw and foreshort-

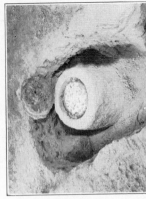

Fig. 38. Above. Stone jar which contained the Disk.

Fig. 39. Below. Over three thousand accurately cut bits of turquoise

Fig. 37 Transferring the famous Turquoise Disk in its stone container from the temple to the hacienda.

Fig. 40

TEMPLE OF THE WARRIORS—CHICHEN ITZA, YUCATAN

After years of stupendous labor had turned a drab mountain of tumbled earth and stone back into its beautiful form of the past.

ened body of the omnipresent Plumed Serpent. This
decoration was worked out by the shaping of the stones,
variation in their color, and by the use of pitchy black
gum to accentuate important features, such as the gaping jaws and the long claws. A blood-red ball of gum
was inserted in the eye socket. The outer rim of the disk
consisted of sixteen petal-shaped blocks of mosaic outlined by brilliant red lacquer.

The plaque is complex to a degree, and beautiful beyond my powers of description. In itself it constitutes
one of the most remarkable discoveries ever made in
America. But, more than this, it is archeologically important because it was found in a definitely recognized
and datable archeological horizon, while the circumstances of its discovery were under expert observation
and control. Moreover, the exquisite quality of turquoise marks the raw material as of probable derivation
from the mines of New Mexico, while the workmanship
is that characteristic of the Valley of Mexico. After a
trip across thousands of miles of desert and jungle it was
laid away beneath a temple which was in its turn des-
tined to be completely buried from view by the greater
structure built on top of it. The chances of the plaque's
eventual so lucky recovery, if computed mathematically,
would stagger an Einstein.

Mr. Ichikawa's reconstruction of the plaque was one
of the most delicate and difficult pieces of work that

have ever been done in the field of American archeology. It came from his hands in perfect condition, and was straightway carried to Mexico City, where it was presented to the delighted government officials and put upon exhibition in the National Museum of that city.

The next year a Congress of Americanists was held in New York. By special request, the honored delegates from Mexico packed the disk to carry with them in order that the people of the United States might have the opportunity of viewing it with their own eyes. And thereby hangs a tale of a series of misfortunes so peculiar that it almost appears as if some malevolent power were bent on wresting the jewel once more from the hands of men.

Off the port of Progresso the ship caught fire, and the passengers were hastily transshipped to the shore. The delegate in charge of the plaque tells that he carried it "next to his heart" and never let it leave him. Nevertheless, the jewel was returned, for the moment, to the very shores of its homeland. Then, when the fire was brought under control, it was found that slight damage had been done, so everybody reëmbarked and the anchor was weighed for further voyage. Hardly was land left behind when a dreadful storm broke. Did the old Plumed Serpent feel his treasure again slipping beyond his reach, and make one last effort toward recovery? All day and all night the wind increased in intensity; water poured from the skies and waves towered above the decks of the great liner. The hatches were battened down, the port holes closed, and in the close, airless ship terrified passengers dumbly waited for almost certain catastrophe. Then the lee shores of Cuba were reached and the boat slid into more quiet, protected waters. Of a sudden the hurricane abated, the rain ceased, and the sun shone again. The dreadful winds which had blown out of the skies of Yucatan were sucked back as suddenly as they had been unleashed. The old gods had been defeated of their prey.

CHAPTER XVIII

The Maya Return to the Wilderness

A FEW final surprises were still left for us. There was nothing so sensational as the turquoise disk, but none the less the material garnered those last weeks was of tremendous importance. We learned a good deal more about the spot of ground covered by the great temple, most of which was completely unexpected, and into those findings we could read a fair amount of good sound Maya history which is substantially corroborated by other evidence.

The Temple of the Warriors was constructed on top of the Buried Temple. That fact obviously dated it as the later structure. However, the discoveries of our last year in Yucatan brought to light other evidences of building on the same spot which complicated the twofold pattern tremendously.

When Earl decided to excavate that great tumbled hill which was, under his hand, to return to being in its old form as the Temple of the Warriors, he never dreamed that the great mound had ever been anything but a unit structure. The happy accident of the exposed column block, which was clasped in spectacular twisted roots and which heralded an entirely unsuspected temple enclosed in the heart of the greater one, put him on the alert. And, not desiring to neglect a single factor, he worked into the core of the smaller pyramid lest yet a third temple be hiding there from view. It was more superstition than science which demanded the labor of him, because he knew that even a series of nested Chinese boxes must come to an end some time, and in all reason the buried pyramid was much too tiny to enshrine a third one in its mass. But he had come so near to missing the first great find that he naturally was over-zealous in pursuit of a second.

His reward in principle was a common one to archeology, for it seems that whenever a digger sets his hand determinedly to the task of finding one particular thing, he almost invariably fails in his immediate objective and stumbles upon quite another—"bigger and better," and hopelessly more complicated.

In the present instance, he had excavated into the Buried Temple from the top and had found nothing. Then, abandoning the pit when it became too deep to be practical, he transferred operations to the base of the structure, and penetrating through the rear wall of the Northwest Colonnade which lay at the base of the Warriors', he completed proof that there was nothing further therein concealed.

But—in the course of the digging he cut through the floor of the Northwest Colonnade, and there, a scant few inches below the polished surface, he came, to his astonishment, upon another floor, also red and smoothly finished. Below this was yet a third, and in them both the sockets where columns had once stood were clearly visible. Evidently the colonnade we knew was but a grandchild of previous, similar buildings, and thus it became painfully evident that stratigraphy was with us once again.

The ensuing problems are too complicated to rehearse. They involved a study of each colonnade in its relation to the two superimposed pyramids, taking into account at the same time its position in relation to the numerous levels of the great central plaster-floored terrace around which many of the important buildings of the city had been placed. Even an account of the bare results is not simple but is perhaps of some interest.

Considering those buildings adjacent to, under, near, or by the Warriors' and the Buried temples, it appeared that the western range of the Court of the Thousand Columns had been constructed first. This was the round-pillared corridor, by the way, that Tuche, the painter, designated as the Whispering Gallery to his neurasthenic sculptor friend.

Later the powers of the city determined that the structure was too short, so they lengthened the colonnade till it passed completely across the front of the area later to be filled by the great Warriors' pyramid.

After this gallery had been in vogue for some time the lords of Chichen Itza were swept up in an even more ambitious building campaign. Most of the new round-columned addition was torn down, and an open-faced gallery supported on square columns with sculptured faces took its place. But, more than this, a pyramid was built in connection with the new hall, and on top of it a temple was dedicated to the Serpent God. From the colonnade a broad staircase led up to the door of the temple. This was the structure we designated as the Buried Temple.

For only fifteen years was this temple in use, when

again a fever of building activity seized upon the rulers of the city. Nor is the reason for such seemingly unrational procedure difficult to find when we recollect the Spanish captain who interviewed the lord of a Maya city and quoted him as saying that "I make a practice of giving my people much to do in order that they may not talk to plan treason against their ruler."

Civil unrest in any empire directly menaces its governing power, but a people whose thoughts are skillfully bent on consistent work, and who, moreover, are too tired at night from the physical labors of the day to do anything but fall sound asleep in the nearest available corner, are not apt to have the energy or leisure to foment rebellion.

The shrewd Itzas were well aware of this, and there is little doubt that the perfect furor of destruction and rebuilding which possessed the city at this time reflected social narcotic measures as much as, if not more than, it did desire for civic betterment.

Once again the wrecking crews fell upon the solid structures, razing the colonnade completely to the ground and filling the empty temple interior with solid masonry, preparatory to incorporating it in the heart of a higher and more massive pyramid. Upon this second pyramid another temple was built, larger and more daringly constructed than any one of the kind ever seen before in the country. This was the building I have described as the Temple of the Warriors, while the new

columned hall lying across the foot of the broad staircase has been called the Northwest Colonnade. (Fig. 40.)

But not even the completion of this magnificent
building unit could still the architectural urge or social
ambition of the Itza king. Almost immediately a new
structure was planned to flank the Warriors' pyramid in
such a manner that sixty-six feet of a beautifully sculptured frieze was obscured by its foundation. I can imagine an architect and several stone cutters who must
have been disgusted beyond measure by such a signal
waste of their efforts.

With this final outrage, the builders would appear to
have given over incessant meddling with the immediate
area and to have transferred their attentions to other
sections of the Court of the Thousand Columns. But
they left for us to find tiny signs which fixed beyond all
dispute the sequence of the five times the place was built
upon.

The initial stages were represented by foundations
only, for the superstructures had been completely torn
away. The last or North Colonnade belongs rightly to
the great court itself and will be completely studied in
connection with excavations which have not yet taken
place. But the two great temples with which our work in
Yucatan was so largely concerned offer a solid basis
whereupon a rather fascinating meshwork of interwoven
deduction and fact reveals an account of old Chichen
Itza as illuminating and as credible as a printed tale.

The earlier building—the Buried Temple—was notably the better of the two, exemplifying conventional, artistic standards of the times. The structure was compact and sturdy, while its painted decorations were bound by the restraints of rigid symbolism. But in the Temple of the Warriors it is possible to see mirrored a radically changing point of view. The building was more daring in conception—indeed, the span of the arch was experimentally made so wide that it is probable that it didn't endure for more than two hundred years. The fresco painting noticeably departs from the traditional both in manner and in subject matter. The freely drawn intimate scenes of daily life have a pronouncedly different flavor from the stiff processions of gods and serpents that parade endlessly across the walls of other buildings. Ancient intricate symbolism was losing ground, the monotonous type of human features gave way to factual portraiture of individual persons, and a very fresh and pleasing naïveté replaced the old abstract grand style.

This much we can read in paint and stone, but therefrom we can deduce a shift in the whole mental make-up of the Maya, for throughout the course of history this has been true. When the craft of art slips the taut leash held by priests and kings, the politics of the times keeps to a parallel course in a growing sense of freedom and self-assertiveness. In this event, when true mental strength lies with the rebellious people, civilization marks a new step in advance. But if only a brutish restlessness is the cause, the culture in question falls inevitably to decay.

With the Maya, that higher knowledge which marked them so signally as the greatest people in America had always been carefully guarded by the priest-king clan. With the fall of these leaders the peculiar genius was gone. Swiftly chaos and degeneration overtook the entire race, preparing the way for easy Spanish victory.

It is probable that the Temple of the Warriors was a manifestation of the last great building cycle of the Maya in Chichen Itza. It was constructed about 1250 A.D. A few generations of rapidly weakening Itza kings must have struggled for retention of their ancient powers, as evidenced by the construction of a few sloppily built small temples. Then an old chronicle has it (and we can read tragic defeat in the few curt words), "The Itzas moved away from Chichen Itza and returned to the land of their fathers." In the southland of Guatemala, about 1450, they set up a little island village for the remnant of their followers, but it was a poor makeshift to replace the beautiful capital of their Yucatan empire.